LENN

LONG BAR PRICE LIST

DOUBLE DIAMOND	1/1
LONG LIFE	1/3
LIGHT	1/3
BROWN	1/3
SPECIAL STOUT	1/4
JOHN BULL	1/2
ARCTIC	1/
LAGER	1/3
GUINNESS	1/3
CIDER OR SHANDY	1/2

SKOL

I ♥ JL

I ♥ JL

LOVE LOVE LOVE LENNON

I ♥ JL

LENNON'S
LENNON'S
LENNON'S LIVERPOOL

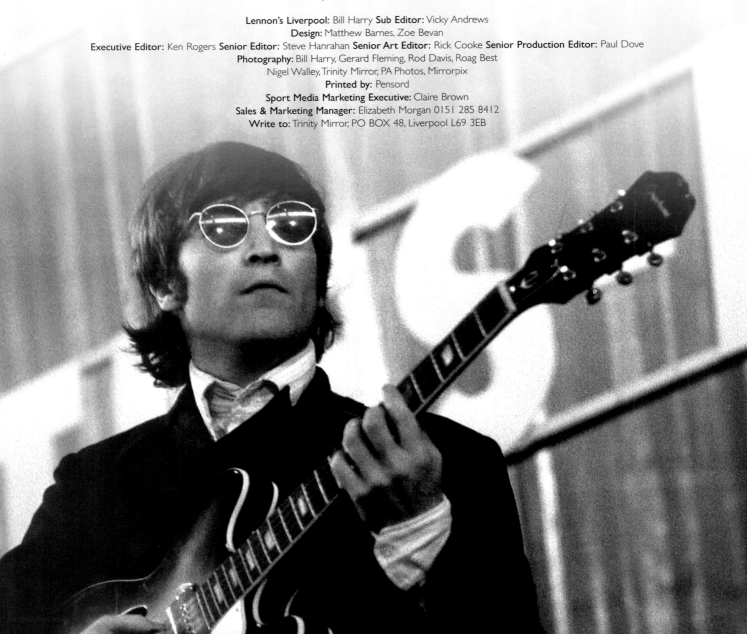

Trinity Mirror Media

Lennon's Liverpool: Bill Harry **Sub Editor:** Vicky Andrews
Design: Matthew Barnes, Zoe Bevan
Executive Editor: Ken Rogers **Senior Editor:** Steve Hanrahan **Senior Art Editor:** Rick Cooke **Senior Production Editor:** Paul Dove
Photography: Bill Harry, Gerard Fleming, Rod Davis, Roag Best
Nigel Walley, Trinity Mirror, PA Photos, Mirrorpix
Printed by: Pensord
Sport Media Marketing Executive: Claire Brown
Sales & Marketing Manager: Elizabeth Morgan 0151 285 8412
Write to: Trinity Mirror, PO BOX 48, Liverpool L69 3EB

INTRODUCTION

John and Bill Harry

John Lennon spent more time in his life in his birthplace Liverpool than anywhere else.

'In My Life' was a song inspired by John's love of the city, which had its origin when a journalist made a remark that John should write songs about his childhood. Soon after, he wrote a song in the form of a long poem reminiscing about his childhood years.

The original version of the lyrics was based on a bus route he used to take in Liverpool, naming various sites seen along the way, including Penny Lane and Strawberry Field.

In writing this brief account of John's life in Liverpool, I could have produced a work several times as large, listing every venue, place he visited, friends he knew – and I must admit I do have all these facts to hand, having been a friend of John's over a 12-year period and studied his life and times for decades. However, I have concentrated on core places to present a general picture of his life in the city.

Of course, there are many different viewpoints relating to relationships, which I call 'The Roshomon Effect' in which various people see the same event through completely different eyes, arriving at another conclusion.

It is natural to understand Julia and Jacquie's picture of Aunt Mimi from the point of view of the mother they loved. Also, for Cynthia Lennon to have a view of Mimi which infuriated June Furlong, who understood the love, devotion and sacrifices this lone woman experienced as she fed, clothed and reared him, while having to keep a tight rein on a rebellious youth. It is easy to see John's love

of his mother Julia, how he found complete freedom in her company, escaping from Mimi's efforts to direct him toward his adult future.

Whether John's father Alf actually deserted him or not is a cause for speculation and opinion, so I've not explored these aspects of John's formative years in the city, concentrating more on the places than the people.

I have, I admit, included my own personal reminiscences, as I grew close to John from 1958 until the last time I was with him in London prior to him moving to New York when he drove Virginia, Yoko and I from the Speakeasy Club to the Bag O' Nails club.

I much appreciate the time and memories given to me by Stan Parkes, Rod Davies, Rod Murray and Roag Best, plus the sterling efforts of Gerard Fleming who spent many a day travelling around Liverpool to provide photographs for the book.

(His groundbreaking website http://liverpooldays.com has a cornucopia of Liverpool images and is well worth a visit). Thanks also to Steve Turner for helping me focus my memory on times experienced at Gambier Terrace.

Also to Ken Rogers of Trinity Mirror whose determination to provide tales of Liverpool glory in published form is commendable, for Peter Grant, an indomitable Lennon fan and all at Trinity Mirror who added in the creation of the book.

For further information on John and to read the stories he wrote for me in Mersey Beat, you'll find them on **www.mersey-beat.com**.

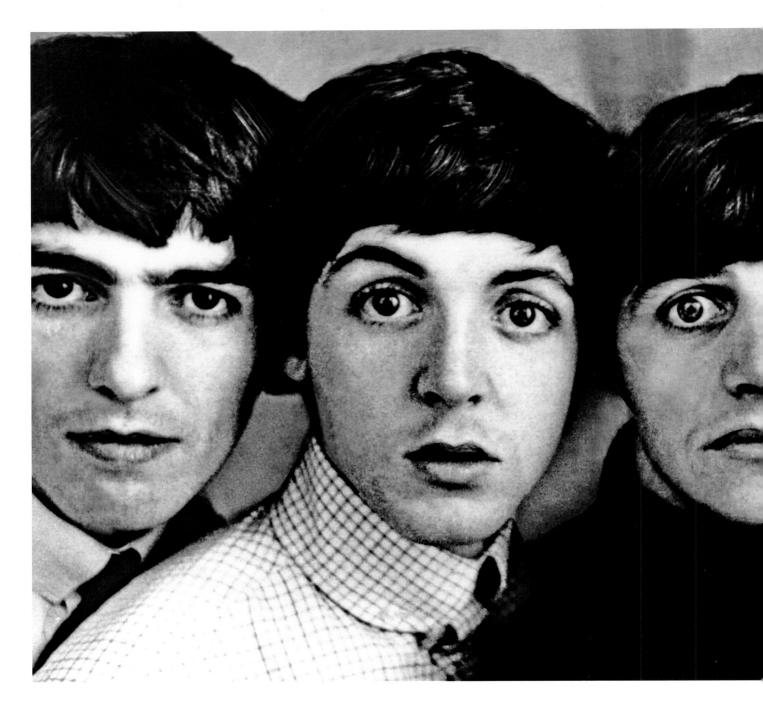

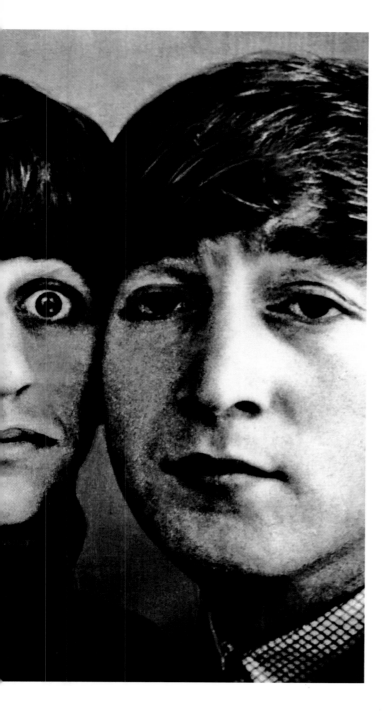

CONTENTS

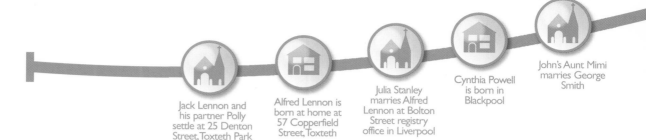

Jack Lennon and his partner Polly settle at 25 Denton Street, Toxteth Park

Alfred Lennon is born at home at 57 Copperfield Street, Toxteth

Julia Stanley marries Alfred Lennon at Bolton Street registry office in Liverpool

Cynthia Powell is born in Blackpool

John's Aunt Mimi marries George Smith

CHAPTER 1
LENNON'S LIVERPOOL

John Lennon was a Liverpool lad. His hopes, his dreams, his aspirations, his genius were all forged in the city of his birth. To understand John, you must understand Liverpool.

Due to its position as one of the world's great seaports over hundreds of years, this sprawling cosmopolitan city had been a melting pot of cultures from the time of the slave trade and was to become a stepping stone for eastern Europeans to travel to America, and a haven for Irish families fleeing the potato famine.

It also sported the first Chinatown in Europe and its equivalent of Harlem lay in the Toxteth area of the city, gathered around Upper Parliament Street. John's own ancestry had its roots in both Ireland and Wales.

DATES AND EVENTS PRIOR TO JOHN'S BIRTH:

On 26 October 1855, John's paternal grandfather, John Lennon, more popularly known as 'Jack', was born. At one time he moved to America where he became a member of Andrew Robertson's Kentucky Minstrels.

On 22 August 1874, George Ernest Stanley, John's maternal grandfather, the son of William Henry Stanley and Eliza Jane Gildea, was born at 120 Salisbury Street, Everton, Liverpool. He became a shipping clerk and in 1906 married Annie Millward.

The couple's first two children, a boy and a girl, both died before reaching the age of three. They then had five daughters Mary Elizabeth (born on 24 April 1906), Elizabeth (born in 1910), Ann Georgina (born in 1912), Judy (Julia) (born at 8 Head Street, Liverpool on 20 March 1914) and Harriet (born in 1916).

On 19 November 1906, Anne Millward and George Edward Stanley were married in a Liverpool parish church.

13

John's paternal grandmother
outside 27 Copperfield Street

In 1901, at the age of 46, John Lennon's paternal grandfather Jack (aka John) was living at 3 Lockhart Street, Toxteth Park, with his 12 year old daughter Mary Elizabeth Lennon. He had previously married Margaret Cowley and, apart from Mary Elizabeth, they had a son Michael.
Margaret died giving birth and Michael also died 15 days later on 19 August 1892.

At Lockhart Street, Jack was also living with Mary 'Polly' Lennon, who was to became his second wife, although they weren't married at this time. His daughter Mary is later believed to have married and settled Down Under.

Then in 1905, the Lennons, Jack (aka John) and his partner Polly settled in 25 Denton Street, Toxteth Park. Jack worked as a freight clerk and their son George was born at this address on 14 August of that year. George was to die in Liverpool in 1956. The couple's second son Herbert was born on 18 April 1908. He died in Conway in 1968.

On 14 December 1912, Alfred Lennon was born at home at 57 Copperfield Street, Toxteth, Liverpool. This was a warren of terraced streets named after characters from Charles Dickens' books.

12 March 1914, Julia Stanley was born in Liverpool, one of the five daughters of George Ernest and Annie Stanley (nee Millward).

John's Uncle Charlie Lennon was born in 1918 and died in Liverpool in 2002. Charlie attended St Silas School, the same school which in later years, Ringo Starr, Billy Fury and Billy Hatton of the Fourmost were to attend.

On 3 December 1938, Julia married Alfred at the Bolton Street registry office in Liverpool, close to the Adelphi Hotel – which isn't the same office where their son would marry Cynthia Powell 24 years later as many books have claimed.

On 10 September 1939, Cynthia Powell was born in Blackpool. Her mother was pregnant when war broke out and her two sons, Tony and Charles, had been evacuated to North Wales. Lillian was sent to lodgings in Blackpool. Her father arrived from Liverpool by train, unaware that his wife was in labour and was sent out to walk in the rain while his daughter was born. Against medical advice, Lillian packed her bags and returned to join her husband in Merseyside.

On 15 September 1939, John's Aunt Mimi married George Smith. The couple had been courting for 10 years and Mimi was 31.

Travelling in style: John and Cynthia fly to New York in 1964

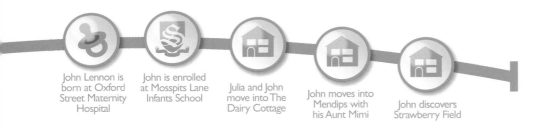
CHAPTER 2
A LEGEND IS BORN

27 COPPERFIELD STREET

Situated in an area in the Dingle, this was also known as Toxteth Park and was a warren of terraced houses where the streets were named after characters from Charles Dickens' novels. John's grandfather Jack (aka John) Lennon and his partner Polly were living at this address when their son Sydney was born on 26 June 1909. The couple also had another son Harold, born in 1911, who died the same year. John Lennon's father Alfred was born in the house on 14 December 1912.

Jack and Polly were eventually married on 27 January 1915 at West Derby Registry Office and for a time moved to Elmore Street in Everton and their daughter Edith was born on 21 March 1915. They returned to Copperfield Street where Charles Lennon was born on 25 November 1918 (Charlie died in Liverpool in 2002). Jack died at his home on 3 August 1921 and was buried in an unmarked grave in Anfield Cemetery.

Mary 'Polly' Lennon had been born Mary Maguire in Liverpool of Irish ancestry and was hired as a housekeeper by Jack Lennon after his first wife Margaret died. Polly gave birth to eight children, six of whom survived. The two babies lost at birth had been baptised Roman Catholics due to the fact that Jack was a Catholic. However, Polly ensured that her other six children were christened as Protestants. She couldn't read nor write, but was said to be very witty and was reputed to be psychic. When her husband died, Polly did not have the financial resources to keep the family together and had to place Alfred and Edith in the Bluecoat School, an orphanage. She died on 30 January 1949.

The area has since been knocked down and new houses built there.

OXFORD STREET MATERNITY HOSPITAL

John was born at on 9 October 1940 at Oxford Street Maternity Hospital, a building now turned into apartments, but sporting a plaque, designed by former Liverpool College of Art student Fred O' Brien, commemorating John's birth.

John's mother Julia had been in labour for 30 hours and the doctors were about to perform a caesarean section, but this proved unnecessary. John's father Alfred was at sea at the time and the baby's first name was chosen in honour of his paternal grandfather and his middle name as a tribute to Winston Churchill, due to the war which was raging.

On 12 October 1940, in the Saturday edition of the *Liverpool Echo*, the following notice appeared:

LENNON – *October 9, in hospital to JULIA (nee Stanley), wife of ALFRED LENNON, Merchant Navy (at sea), a son – 9 Newcastle Road.*

Most books about John wrongly assert that he was born during a German air raid on the city, which is not the case. This misinformation first appeared in Hunter Davies' authorised biography of the group in which he wrote: "Julia was admitted to the Maternity Hospital in Oxford Street to have her baby. He was born during a heavy air raid on October 9, 1940 at seven in the morning and he was called John Winston Lennon."

This entry was actually changed in a later edition of the biography in which Hunter wrote: "He was born during a heavy air raid on 9 October 1940, at 6.30 in the evening and was called John Winston Lennon."

Ged Flemming

THIS IS NOT HERE

To Julia Lennon, née Stanley, a son

John Lennon

(1940-80)
born here in the former
Liverpool Maternity Hospital
6.30pm 9 October 1940

PLAQUE PLACED BY
NORTHERN DESIGN UNIT
9 OCTOBER 2000

"UPPERMOST IN MIMI'S THOUGHTS WAS CONCERN FOR HER SISTER, MINGLED WITH DELIGHT THAT A BOY HAD ENTERED THE OVERWHELMINGLY FEMALE STANLEY FAMILY."

The authorised biography was obviously used as a reference in many others that followed:

"John Lennon was born on 9 October 1940. During one of the fiercest night raids by Hitler's Luftwaffe on Liverpool."
Philip Norman, *Shout*

"John Winston Lennon was born during one of those massive air raids on 9 October 1940 in a maternity home in Oxford Street."
Peter Brown, *The Love You Make*

"The planes of the German Luftwaffe flew overhead on 9 October 1940, dropping bombs on the city. It was the night John Winston Lennon was born."
Carole Lynn Corbin, *Lennon*

"John Winston Lennon was born during one of those massive air raids on 9 October 1940 in a maternity home in Oxford Street."
Tom Stockdale, *John Lennon*

"John Lennon entered and left this life amid smoke, flame and flying steel. When Julia Lennon gave birth to him on the night of October 9 1940 at the height of the Battle of Britain, the Luftwaffe was unloading another firestorm onto His Majesty's dockyards in Liverpool."
Henry W Sullivan, *The Beatles With Lacan*

"It was into this world of shifting, confused and lonely people that John Lennon was born at 6.30 in the evening of 9 October 1940 at the Oxford Street Maternity Hospital, Liverpool. Outside a heavy bombing raid was shaking the city."
Ray Connolly, *John Lennon 1940-1980*

"Indeed, when John Winston Lennon – the middle name was in honour of British Prime Minister Churchill – was born on October 9, 1940, Liverpool was in the middle of a punishing bombing raid."
Mark Hertsgaard, *A Day In The Life*

"October 9th 1940, saw a particularly fierce spate of night raids, but this was the last thing on the mind of young Julia Lennon as she lay in Liverpool's Oxford Street Maternity Home. With bombs falling around the hospital, Julia gave birth to a boy."
Terry Burrows, *The Beatles*

Ged Fleming

The former Oxford Street Maternity Hospital where John was born

"An air raid was at its height when John Winston Lennon was born at 7 o' clock on the morning of 9 October."
Julia Baird, *John Lennon My Brother*

Now why does Julia, John's half-sister, state that the birth took place at 7 when all other sources report 6.30, with even Davies' official biography now claiming the 6.30 time? The latter seems the most appropriate because of John's obsession with the number 9, but I have seen John's birth certificate and the time of the birth was not recorded. On the other hand, other reports state that he was born at 7:04pm!

One of the main sources of material for people who write books about John or the Beatles is Philip Norman's *Shout.* This is a beautifully crafted book and Norman is an exceptional writer. He also enlivens his writing with hyperbole, imagining and visualising scenes and colouring them with a writer's licence to exaggerate.

While Davies just mentioned a 'heavy air raid', Philip colours the entire scene, making it dramatic and exciting: "Sometimes the whole audience would crown out into the foyer to look across the black acropolis of St George's Hall, to a sky flashing white, then dark again as more bombs pummelled the port and the river." He has Mimi Stanley running two miles to the hospital "with Liverpool aflame." Arriving at the hospital she holds John in her arms 20 minutes after the birth:

"Just then a landmine fell directly outside the hospital."

In the early 1980s I met Helen Simpson, an archivist who had formerly worked at Merseyside's Maritime Museum. She enjoyed her post and began researching the local archives.
She phoned me up to say that reports in the *Liverpool Echo* confirmed that there was a lull in the bombing of Merseyside on 9

October 1940. There had been raids previously and they were to resume in the near future, but when John was born, there was no bombing raid!

This seemed to be confirmed by David Stuart Ryan in his book *John Lennon's Secret*. Ryan spent some time in Liverpool researching the book, in which he writes:

"The evening John Lennon was born on October 9 1940, at 6.30pm in Liverpool's Oxford Street Hospital, there were not – as he liked to imply – any bombs falling. There had been an unexpected interruption which was quickly shattered by the following evening when the docks were again hammered by German bombs."

Barry Miles, in his entry for 9 October 1940 in his book *The Beatles: A Diary* wrote: "John Winston Lennon born at Oxford Street Maternity Hospital to Alfred Lennon and Julia Lennon, nee Stanley. Contrary to other reports, there was no Luftwaffe raid that night."

Ron Jones in *The Beatles Liverpool* writes: "Most accounts of John's birth tell of Aunt Mimi dodging shrapnel through the bomb-torn streets of Liverpool to see the new baby who had to be placed under the bed during an air raid. It is a nice, whimsical, oft-told tale, but a tall one for all that. Official war records confirm that the Luftwaffe gave Liverpool a miss that particular night."

Philip Norman in his acclaimed biography *John Lennon: A Life*, completely altered the view of John's birth he had originally documented in *Shout*, also providing an insight into why Mimi thought there was a raid that night:

"But on the night of 9-10 October, the Luftwaffe unaccountably stayed away. As Mimi hurried towards Oxford Street, she would have undoubtedly seen the results of previous bombing, in rubble, shattered glass and white-haired ARP wardens. In later visits to Julia, the situation could have been as she remembered that first night, with a land mine falling next to the hospital and the new baby being wrapped in a rough blanket and put under his mother's bed for safety. Uppermost in Mimi's thoughts on 9 October was concern for her sister, mingled with delight that a boy had entered the overwhelmingly female Stanley family. Possibly it was the strength of her own emotion when she first held her nephew in her arms that helped give the scene its apocalyptic quality in her memory."

Although it now seems clear that there was no air raid on Liverpool during the night of 9 October 1940, there still seemed to be some confusion regarding the raids prior to and after that date.

I'd discussed this situation with Rod Davis, former member of John's original skiffle group the Quarry Men, which Rod had re-formed and he informed me that he had researched that particular aspect.

He told me that he'd read books stating that John had been born at the hospital on 9 October 1940 around 6.30pm "during a heavy air raid – a detail which is sometimes attributed to John's Aunt Mimi."

During his appearances with the Quarry Men he often found himself asked to debunk some of the myths and decided to investigate the night of John's birth by researching copies of the *Liverpool Echo* dating from early October 1940 to read the reports on the air raids on the city.

Rod drove to the Newspaper Archive and obtained bound volumes of the *Echo* covering October 1940. The issue of Wednesday 9 October mentioned raids "on several towns in the South and South West England" on the previous night.

He comments, "Then I turned to the edition for Thursday 10 November in which I would have expected from the Echo reports I had already read, to find details of raids on Merseyside which had happened in the previous 24 hours, the day on which John Lennon was born." He also read a German communiqué covering events on Wednesday 9 October which also covered German raids, of which none were on Merseyside.

His conclusion: "So it would appear that according to both the Echo and the German Communiqué that there was no air raid activity over Liverpool on Wednesday 9 October."
He adds: "There were, however, raids on Thursday 10th which were reported in the Echo on Friday 11 October on page 8 under the headline 'Raiders split by Mersey defences – only a few got through.'"

The home in Newcastle Road where John Lennon spent the first few years of his life

9 NEWCASTLE ROAD, WAVERTREE

When Stan Parkes – the elder statesman of the Lennon clan and the one John looked up to like an elder brother – was chosen to unveil the English Heritage blue plaque outside Mendips, the former home of Aunt Mimi and John, he was to impart a piece of family history:

"A wealthy Welsh relative left our Great Grandmother a tidy sum of money, so she bought five or six little properties dotted all around where the Anglican Cathedral stands today. She rented these properties out and when they became vacant she would put our Grandmother into them to look after them until a new client could be found. Hence all our mothers – the five Stanley sisters, were all born at different addresses.

"As you all know, Liverpool took a hammering with the heavy bombing all around the dock area. A friend and neighbour of our Grandparents had two properties at Newcastle Road. He stated that things were getting very dangerous with the bombing and he was going back to live in one of his houses at Penny Lane and I think you should come too and live in my other property, which they decided to do.

"The majority of the Stanley Sisters were married from the 9 Newcastle Road address; hence we all came to live in and around Woolton."

The property was a two-bedroom terraced house in the Wavertree area. It was the cause of some controversy in 1981 when an estate agent advertised it as John's birthplace, offering it for sale at a hugely inflated price. John's Aunt Mimi said that it was her parent's home where John had spent a couple of months when he was a baby. This was actually the Stanley home.

George and Annie Stanley had originally lived in Huskisson Street and their first two children, a boy and a girl, died before their third birthdays. They then had five healthy daughters: Mary Elizabeth, Elizabeth, Ann Georgina, Julia and Harriet. The family next moved on to the house in Newcastle Road. Julia lived here during the years of her courtship with Freddie Lennon and on their wedding night, Julia returned to Newcastle Road while Freddie went into lodgings and then off to sea.

John was reared at this address during the first few years of his life. He was later to recall that it was "the first place I remember . . . red brick . . . front room never used, always curtains drawn . . . picture of horse and carriage on the wall. There were only three bedrooms upstairs, one on the front of the street, one in the back and one teeny little room in the middle."

During this time Freddie was away at sea and Julia was able to collect some money from his earning from the Seamen's Mission. However, this money stopped when it was reported that Freddie had gone AWOL in New York.

Julia's sister Mimi, who had married George Smith, was renting a house in Vale Road, Woolton. George owned a small cottage.

It has been suggested that as Julia liked going out and having a good time at night, the baby John was left alone in the dark on so many occasions that it traumatised him and left him in fear of the dark for the rest of his life.

I can't vouch for the validity of this, but Stan Parkes tells me that it was George Stanley who was to ask Mimi to take John away from his mother. This occurred when Julia was living with Bobby Dykins.

It was said that Mimi complained that Julia was an unfit mother and brought a social worker to their flat, demanding that John be taken away from Julia and given to her. The social worker pointed out that a son should remain with his mother.

However, when it was discovered that there was no bed for John and that he actually slept in the double bed with the couple, it was decided that he had to move in with his Aunt Mimi until they could find a bigger flat. But they never did.

MOSSPITS LANE INFANTS SCHOOL

Situated in Mosspits Lane, Wavertree, Liverpool 15, this was the first infants school that John attended. While he was still living in Newcastle Road, he was enrolled in the primary school on 12 November 1945.

From all accounts, the five-year old John apparently bullied a young neighbour, Polly Hipshaw, who also attended the school. It was said that as a result, in April 1946 John was expelled for his disruptive behaviour and on 6 May was enrolled at Dovedale Road Junior School. However, no report regarding an expulsion had been made in the school's logbook, which only reported he had 'left district.' The latter paints the true picture as John had now moved in with his Aunt Mimi and she picked the Dovedale primary as it was close to Mendips.

Mosspits Junior School in Wavertree, the first infants school that John Lennon attended

DOVEDALE ROAD PRIMARY SCHOOL

This children's school was situated in Dovedale Road, Liverpool 18, three miles from Mendips. Dovedale Primary was the school John's Aunt Mimi picked for her nephew to attend. Some reports have hinted that he was expelled from his previous primary school, Mosspits Lane Infants School, for alleged bad behaviour, and there is some evidence to show that he proved unruly at the time. However, when he attended Mosspits he was living at Newcastle Road and it was the closest school to the Stanley household. When he moved in with his Aunt Mimi, Dovedale Road Primary was much closer to their home.

John was enrolled at his new infant's school on 6 May 1946. At a parent's meeting the head teacher Mr Bolt told Mimi, "There's no need to worry about him. He's as sharp as a needle. He can do anything as long as he chooses to do it."

John admitted to being reasonably well behaved at Dovedale in comparison with the rebellious attitude he was to take when he enrolled at Quarry Bank School.

He said, "I'd been honest at Dovedale, if nothing else, always owning up. But I began to realise that I was foolish."

However, he was also later to confess that at Dovedale he had a gang who indulged in shoplifting and "pulling girls knickers down". He also said that the parents and even the teachers hated him.

Of other boys who tried to challenge him, he commented, "I used to beat them up if they were small enough but I'd use long words and confuse them if they were bigger. What mattered was that I stayed in charge."

Another school pupil at the time was Jimmy Tarbuck, who became a popular comedian. Jimmy said that even when John was a child he was an oddball. Peter Harrison, one of George Harrison's elder brothers, was also in the same class as John. George himself attended Dovedale but was three years behind John. In 1948 John transferred to the Junior Boys School at Dovedale and remained there until his 11-plus examination in 1952.

Above: Pupils from Dovedale circa 1952 – John Lennon is back row, sixth from left

Dovedale Road Primary School, the school that John's Aunt Mimi picked for her nephew to attend

23

Above: John Lennon with his mother Julia
Right: Pictured as a young schoolboy

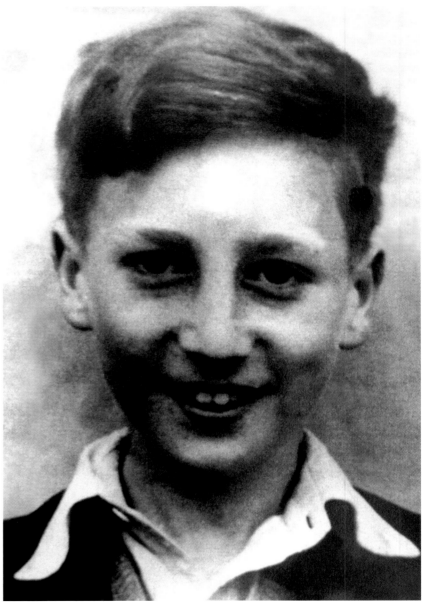

"JULIA USED TO SING A SONG TO JOHN WHICH INCLUDED THE WORDS, *WANT TO KNOW A SECRET?"*

THE DAIRY COTTAGE

This semi-detached cottage in High Street, Woolton, was owned by George Smith, who was married to John's Aunt Mimi. When Alfred Lennon became head waiter on a ship leaving Liverpool a month prior to John's second birthday, Mimi suggested that Julia and John could move into this two-bedroom semi-detached cottage.

Julia was keen on the idea, as it would enable her to enjoy a degree of freedom while Mimi was pleased that it meant that John would be closer to the Mendips house.

In some ways it wasn't an ideal move because George Stanley had a degree of control over Julia when she lived in the family home in Newcastle Road. In her new abode, with her husband away at sea and no longer being under her parents eye, she began going out on her own for the first time, to pubs and dances. When Alfred returned from sea for a brief period in 1943, he noticed the changes in his wife. Then he had to leave again for an 18-month period at sea in July.

However, Stan Parkes used to visit Julia and John at the Cottage and said he never ever saw her with a drink in her hand.

It was while they were at the Cottage that Julia used to sing a song from a Disney film to him, which included the words "Want to know a secret?"
John had that song in mind many years later when he wrote *Do You Want to Know a Secret.*

Julia and John were in the Cottage for several months. Then, in 1943, Annie Stanley died. George didn't want to remain in Newcastle Road after that and moved in with some other relatives, inviting Julia and Alf to return to Newcastle Road with John.

Some years later, the cottage was occupied by Julia's sister Harriet, her husband Norman and their son David.

When Julia was killed in the car accident in Menlove Avenue, her daughters Julia and Jacqueline weren't initially told about it and were sent to stay with Mater, Burt and Stanley in Edinburgh. Julia's partner Bobby couldn't bear the thought of remaining in Springwood with all its happy memories and moved out.

Many years later the sisters discovered that they had been made wards of court and their father could no longer look after them, although he had once had them fostered. Following their return to Liverpool they joined Harriet, Norman and David in the dairy cottage, although they still weren't informed that their mother had died – some considerable time was to pass before Norman revealed the tragic information to them.

Stan was to tell me: "The Dairy Cottage was the main living quarters for the Dairy Maid for Uncle George's Dairy Farm. It was cramped in as much as the two bedrooms were not suitable for two girl cousins and cousin David to sleep in the same bedroom together. Otherwise there were two living room quarters, a back kitchen area and a hallway. It was all part of the main Dairy Farm set up."

The Salvation Army orphanage in Beaconsfield Road, where John Lennon used to go to garden parties as a child

STRAWBERRY FIELD

A Salvation Army orphanage situated in Beaconsfield Road, Liverpool 25, where the young John Lennon used to play in its environs. There was originally a large Victorian mansion on the site, but that was knocked down and replaced by a modern building. Together with his mates Pete Shotton and Nigel Whalley, John used to visit the annual fêtes, which took place in the grounds of Strawberry Field each summer.

The several acres of grounds were well wooded and ideal for John and his mates to play in. The garden fêtes enabled them to sell lemonade bottles for a penny each. They later admitted to a habit of stealing items from stalls during those bittersweet days, which resounded to the throb of the Salvation Army band.

His Aunt Mimi recalled: "There was something about the place that always fascinated John. He could see it from his window, and he loved going to the garden party they had each year. He used to hear the Salvation Army band, and he would pull me along, saying, "Hurry up, Mimi — we're going to be late!"

The memories provided his inspiration for his song 'Strawberry Fields Forever'. Commenting on the number, Paul McCartney said that Strawberry Field "was the place right opposite John's house where he used to go and play in the garden kind of thing, so it was a kind of magical childhood place for him. We transformed it into the sort of psychedelic dream, so it was everybody's magical childhood place, instead of just ours."

John was to say, "Strawberry Fields is a real place . . . I moved in with my auntie who lived in the suburbs in a nice semi-detached place with a small garden and doctors and lawyers and that ilk living around — not the poor slummy kinds of image that was projected in all the Beatles stories . . . near that home was Strawberry Fields, a house near a boys' reformatory where I used to go to garden parties as a kid with my friends Nigel and Pete. We would go there and hang out and sell lemonade bottles for a penny. We always had fun at Strawberry Fields. Also that's where I got the name. But I used it as an image, 'Strawberry Fields Forever.'

John was later to name a boat after the place and his Aunt Mimi was to buy a tree to be planted in Strawberry Field in memory of John.

Mendips on Menlove Avenue, where John went
to live with his Aunt Mimi and Uncle George

251 MENLOVE AVENUE

At this address was 'Mendips', which was the name of the semi-detached house where John went to live with his Aunt Mimi and Uncle George in 1945. It was named after the Welsh hills and was a pleasant house, built in the 1930s, with leaded windows and a porch, in which John spent many hours practicing with his guitar.

John was reared by Mary Elizabeth Smith, affectionately known as his Aunt Mimi, and was one of Julia Stanley's four sisters.

Mimi left home at the age of 19 to become a resident trainee nurse at Woolton convalescent hospital and eventually became a nursing sister in charge of a ward full of mentally handicapped patients. Later on she became a private secretary to a local businessman.

Mimi married dairy farmer George Smith on September 15 1939, but the couple had no children of their own and Mimi insisted that Julia let her take care of John, as she believed that Julia was neglecting him. Julia agreed and John went to live with his aunt from the age of five. Yet she was to say that it wasn't true that he was that age when he came to her. "I brought him up from a few weeks old until he was 21. My husband George adored John just as though he was his own son.

"All this talk about John's hard upbringing in a Liverpool slum is a fantasy. He wasn't pampered but he had the best of everything we could provide."

She was to also say: "To tell you the truth, when he was born I nearly went off me nut! A boy! Because we were all girls."

Recalling when she rushed to the hospital on 9 October 1940 and saw John for the first time, she said, "Do you believe in fate because I knew the moment I saw John in that hospital that I was the one to be his mother, not Julia. Does that sound awful? It isn't really, because Julia accepted it as something perfectly natural. She used to say, 'You're his real mother. All I did was give birth.'"

It was Mimi who chose the name John and Julia who chose the name Winston. Julia was feeling patriotic and gave him the middle name in tribute to Winston Churchill, then Britain's wartime leader.

Mimi enjoyed rearing him and recalled how she used to send him off to bed with a panda under one arm and a teddy bear under the other. She said he sang himself to sleep every night.

"We so enjoyed having him, they were the best years of my life bringing him up."

Initially, John had both Mimi and her husband George Smith looking after him. John's Uncle George was a father figure in his early life and was six foot tall. George was a dairyman, like his father and grandfather, and delivered milk from a horse-drawn float in the Woolton Village area.

George had been courting Mimi Stanley for ten years and they were finally married when she was 33 years old. He was called into service, but discharged three years later and went to work in an aircraft factory in Speke. The couple moved into Mendips.

George's ambition had been to become an architect, but this dream came to an end when he was expelled from school and entered his father's dairy business.

He was particularly fond of John and when the boy was four and a half years old, taught him to read by reciting the headlines from the *Liverpool Echo* to him. He also taught John how to draw and paint and bought him his first mouth organ.

Mimi was to say, "My husband George adored John just as though he was his own son. And like all dads he spoiled him. Sometimes when John had done something wrong and I sent him up to his room, I'd find George creeping upstairs with the Beano, John's favourite comic, and a bar of chocolate."

When John was 14 he was away on holiday at Durness, Scotland with his Aunt Elizabeth. At Mendips, George suddenly began to vomit blood and was rushed to Sefton General Hospital where he died of a haemorrhage produced by cirrhosis of the liver. John wasn't told immediately. When he arrived home a few days later and asked for his Uncle George, Mimi told him the tragic news. John went upstairs. He was to say, "Then my cousin Leila arrived and she came upstairs as well, we both had hysterics. We just laughed and laughed. I felt very guilty afterwards."

George was 52 years of age when he died on 5 June 1955.

John Lennon with
his Aunt Mimi

make words up about me in the song he was singing. He sang, 'Mimi's coming down the path.'"

Of his years with his auntie, John commented, "I never forgave my auntie for not treating me like a genius. It was obvious to me. I was different. I used to tell her not to throw my poetry out because she would regret it when I was famous – but she still threw it out."

Mimi admitted that she didn't approve of Paul or George when she first saw them. When he talked about his group, she was to comment, "I did everything I could to talk John out of it. I thought he was daft. Stick to art, I told him. But he was right – although I still say he would have made a big success in art even if he hadn't made quite as much money. Anytime I tried to reason with him, or when I got annoyed with him, he'd just answer in that nonsense talk of his and it made me laugh so I always lost the argument. He does that with interviewers, too."

She was also to say, "When he lived with me, he was always very considerate. When he first got mixed up in the beat business in Liverpool he was out in cafés till all hours. Finally I told him that no boy of mine was going to hang around cafés late at night, and he was never very late after that."

When the Beatles became successful, John bought her a bungalow for £25,000, 'Harbour View,' at 126 Panorama Road, Poole, Dorset on 3 August 1965 where she remained for the rest of her life. The bungalow was situated in Sandbanks, an exclusive peninsula at Pool Harbour and John said it was, "The most beautiful place I have ever seen."

Although Mimi Smith seemed quite content in Mendips, John bought her a luxury bungalow near Bournemouth and she moved south. John asked her not to sell Mendips as he couldn't bear the thought of his childhood home in the hands of someone else, but Mimi disagreed, feeling that a house shouldn't be left empty.

He tried to persuade her to spend six months of each year at Mendips and the rest of the year in Poole, but she felt that any break must be a clean one and the house was sold to a doctor.

Once in Poole, she said, "Before I moved here, when I lived in Liverpool, sometimes there would be 50 girls outside the house.

Mimi then had to raise John on her own. She was to say, "I would sometimes rant and rave at him, but deep down he knew I loved him and that he loved me. We were very close."

On the historic day that John met Paul, Mimi couldn't find John. So she went along to the fête by herself where she met some of her sisters and other members of the family. It wasn't until John actually went on stage that she knew he was even taking part in the fête.

She was to say, "I was having a cup of tea in the refreshment tent. Suddenly, in the midst of everything, came this . . . this eruption of noise. Everyone had drained away from were I stood, in the field next door. And there on the stage I saw them, John and that Shotton.

"John saw me standing there with my mouth open. He started to

Of course, I couldn't just let them stay out there, so I'd bring them in for tea. And you know they'd pinch the cups for souvenirs."

She died at her home at the age of 88 on Friday 6 December 1991 and Yoko, Sean and Cynthia attended her cremation at Poole Crematorium in Dorset on Thursday 12 December, while Paul, George and Ringo sent bouquets. The message on Paul's wreath read: "Dear Mimi, it's great to know you in life. You were an exceptional woman, and loved by many of us. God bless, Paul, Linda and children."

There were a total of 30 mourners, who also included John's half-sisters Julie and Jacqueline.

Over the years Mendips has become something of a shrine — a special sign had to be erected outside the house: "Official Notice. Private. No Admission. Merseyside County Council."

In 2000 a special blue plaque was displayed outside the house, which is now run by English Heritage who organise visits to the property. One of their blurbs reads: 'Visit the bedroom where John Lennon did his dreaming.' They have little framed portraits of Brigitte Bardot in the room.

In fact, what John had on his bedroom ceiling was a life-size image of Bardot in her lingerie, by Sam Letts, which had been included as weekly parts in the Reveille newspaper.

Mimi Smith at her home in Bournemouth in 1981

Ged Fleming

Aunt Mimi's bedroom and the living room at Mendips

"JOHN PAID A FINAL VISIT TO BLOMFIELD ROAD IN 1970 WHEN HE TOOK YOKO ON A NOSTALGIC VISIT TO HIS OLD HAUNTS IN LIVERPOOL"

I BLOMFIELD ROAD

When Julia Lennon began living with John 'Bobby' Dykins and gave birth to a daughter, Julia, the family lodged with Julia's father George 'Pop' Stanley at 9 Newcastle Road in Wavertree.

The house was a rented one and when Pop died in 1949 the owner put it up for sale. Julia and Bobby couldn't afford to buy it and as Julia was pregnant with their second daughter Jacquie, the council provided them with accommodation at Blomfield Road on the Springwood council estate in Garston, Liverpool. This was approximately only a few miles distance from Menlove Avenue where John was living with his Aunt Mimi. It was a corner council house semi with large gardens where children could play and an allotment (now gone) at the rear.

When John was in his teens his cousin Stan Parkes reunited him with his mother, and John began visiting Blomfield Road frequently. Young Julia had a double bed, so whenever John stayed overnight, Jacqui would join her and John would sleep in Jacqui's room.

When the girls were in bed at night they said they could often hear John and their mother chatting and playing records downstairs when their father was working late. They recall they were mainly Elvis Presley records such as 'Hound Dog', 'Heartbreak Hotel' and 'Jailhouse Rock'. Elvis was such an influence on the household that they named their new cat Elvis - and then discovered their mistake when she later gave birth to kittens!

On a number of occasions John would bring along Paul McCartney, George Harrison, Pete Shotton and Ivan Vaughan and they would rehearse crammed into the tiny bathroom.

At approximately 7pm on 15 July 1958, after the family had had tea, young Julia, who was playing in the garden with friends, noticed her mother leave to visit Mimi. Her sister Jacquie was in bed and John and her father were in the kitchen chatting. It was John who opened the door when a policeman called later that evening to inform them that Julia had been killed in an accident. John said: "It was awful, like some dreadful film where they ask you if you're the victim's son and all that. Well, I was, and I can tell you it was absolutely the worst night of my entire life."

Dykins could no longer bear to live at Blomfield Road and rented off the property, while his daughters were taken away to live with their Aunt Harrie.

John paid a final visit to Blomfield Road in 1970 when he took Yoko on a nostalgic visit to his old haunts in Liverpool. They drove up to Blomfield Road in their white Rolls Royce and were shown around the premises by Georgie Wood, who had taken over the lease from Dykins.

Ged Fleming

Quarry Bank High School in Allerton

John Lennon joins Quarry Bank High School in 1952

John forms his first skiffle group with Pete Shotton

The Quarry Men are formed

Lennon and McCartney meet at Woolton Parish Church summer fete

CHAPTER 3
SCHOOL DAYS

QUARRY BANK HIGH SCHOOL

A school located in Harthill Road, Allerton, Liverpool 18. It was originally founded on 11 January 1922. The first headmaster was R F Bailey, another was a Mr George Harrison! When John attended the headmaster was E R Taylor who was present for the first five years of John's time at the school and he was replaced by William Pobjoy during John's final year at Quarry Bank.

Pobjoy, incidentally, was an influential headmaster and banned corporal punishment from the school in 1961, many years ahead of it being adopted nationwide.

Former pupils had included Labour ministers Peter Shore and Bill Rodgers, actor Derek Nimmo, singer Michael Cox and later pupils included horror writer Clive Barker and Douglas Bradley ('Pinhead' in the Hellraiser movies). The most famous pupil was undoubtedly John Lennon, who began to attend Quarry Bank in 1952, five years after it had become a grammar school, having passed the 11-plus exam. Some members of his former gang had moved to different schools, Nigel Walley to the Bluecoat and Ivan Vaughan to Liverpool Institute. Fortunately, John's best pal Pete Shotton joined him at Quarry Bank and the two were inseparable as 'Lotton and Shennon'.

The school motto was: 'Ex Hoc Metallo Virtutem, meaning 'From This Rough Metal We Forge Virtue.' When John enrolled at the school on 4 September 1952, he recalled, "I looked at all the hundreds of new kids and thought 'Christ, I'll have to fight my way through all this lot.'"

Ged Fleming

"JOHN'S THIRD YEAR REPORT READ: 'HOPELESS. RATHER A CLOWN IN CLASS. A SHOCKING REPORT. HE IS WASTING OTHER PUPILS' TIME.'"

Right: A young Rod Davis, John Lennon's Quarry Bank friend and an original member of The Quarry Men, an outfit he still performs with today

John's academic record was not one he could be proud of and he was noted for the antics he took part in with his best friend, Pete Shotton. His third year report read: "Hopeless. Rather a clown in class. A shocking report. He is wasting other pupils' time."

Incoming headmaster William E Pobjoy reputedly took an interest in the rebellious pupil and although his exam results were disastrous, John was able to find a place at Liverpool College of Art, with Mr Pobjoy's recommendation. He left in 1957, having failed in all seven of the O level examinations that he sat for in June 1957.

He even failed in the art section, recalling, "I was never neat. I used to mix all the colours together. We had one question which said do a picture of 'travel'. I drew a picture of a hunchback with warts all over him."

Ever since Popjoy entered the school he had heard of John's disruptive nature, but still believed he could achieve something and was conscious of John's flair for art. When John's Aunt Mimi met the headmaster prior to John leaving the school, she recalled, "Pobjoy asked me what I was going to do with him. I said, what are you going to do with him. You've had him for five years."

Popjoy once said of John, "I asked him to write out for me what his principal interests were and he began with salmon fishing." And regarding John's group: "In those days he hadn't thought of making money from it. For instance he came to me and asked for permission to play with the Quarry Men in the interval of the sixth form dance. I said I'd think about it and reluctantly agreed. But it never occurred to him to ask for money."

Pobjoy said he would recommend John for the Liverpool College of Art if Mimi would be prepared to pay for him during his first year.

She agreed and on the last day of term, 17 July, 1957, he wrote a personal reference for John, a sort of left-handed compliment: "He has been a trouble spot for many years in discipline but has somewhat mended his ways. Requires the sanction of 'losing a job' to keep him on the rails. But I believe he is not beyond redemption and he could really turn out a fairly responsible adult who might go far."

With the demise of grammar schools and the advent of the comprehensive, the name was changed to Calderstones Community Comprehensive School – Quarry Bank Wing.

Interestingly enough, Quarry Bank High School is where the seeds of the Beatles were sewn when John formed his first skiffle group, in late September 1956. They initially comprised John Lennon, his friend Pete Shotton who'd constructed a tea chest bass using an old broom handle and a piece of string and Bill Smith on washboard. Eric Griffiths next joined them on guitar.

Rod Davis then joined them on banjo followed by Colin Hanton on drums, although by October 1956 they dispensed with Smith's services because he never seemed to turn up for rehearsals and replaced him with Len Garry. Occasionally, another friend, Ivan Vaughan, would stand in as tea chest bass player.

There is some dispute as to whether the initial name, albeit for only a week or so, was the Blackjacks.

Rod Davis and Len Garry remember the name; Pete Shotton disagrees although Nigel Walley recalls the name the Blackjacks was used for a very short time. Pete also says he formed the group with John, while Eric Griffiths disputes this, saying that both he and John went to a guitar teacher in Hunts Cross with the intention of learning to play and then forming a group – although they only had one or two lessons.

I asked former member Rod Davis, who also attended Quarry Bank with John for his recollections. He told me: "It is my distinct recollection that the first name was the Blackjacks. I feel that it came from the fact that we wore black jeans and white shirts and that the tea chest was painted black. I can't remember if we played any gigs as the Blackjacks, but the name certainly did not last very long, maybe a couple of weeks at the very most.

"I was never in the same class as John at Quarry Bank. However, I was in the same house. The school was divided into nine houses. The three first year forms, called 1R, 1F and 1B (the initials came from the first headmaster Mr R F Bailey) and they were called Bailey House.

"From the second year upwards you went into the house called after the area of Liverpool in which you lived. This had many advantages: you got to know other Quarry Bank boys who were not in your form but lived in your area. When we went to the swimming baths we went to those in Woolton and then could walk home (other houses went to their local baths), and it generated some kind of team spirit based on more than simply randomly allocating boys to different houses with no other affiliation.

"When school began in the morning we went to our 'house rooms', normally two rooms per house, for 15 minutes or so and we registered and then went into assembly as a house. After assembly we then went to lessons in forms. At the end of the day we would go back to our house rooms for 'prep' (this was very public school) or 'house period' as it came to be called.

"This was when I saw the 'Daily Howl' which John would pass around. It was written in what we called a 'block exercise book', half an inch thick, which was issued by the school for taking notes.

"Occasionally you could acquire one of these for personal use and they were highly prized. They were either blank, lined or with graph paper inside, I can't remember what the Daily Howl was produced on. It was very funny and we frequently got 'told off' for laughing at it. It contained jokes and drawings and spoof news items, just the sort of thing which John produced later.

"I don't remember John as a bully, but he could certainly keep his end up in a fight.

"At Quarry Bank I was part of a group of boys who took three or four GCE's at the end of year four and then started on A level work in the fifth year. I had been in 4 Science for a month or two and then changed to 4 Arts because I wanted to do Spanish and French. There was also a 4B and a 4C. I think that by this time John was in 4C but I could be wrong.

"When I joined the Quarry Men I was in a form which was called Lower Sixth Transitus Arts (what a mouthful that was) and I was never a member of a proper fifth year form, but there were only

Paul McCartney makes his public debut with the Quarry Men with John Lennon, Colin Hanton, Len Garry and Eric Griffiths

about eight of us, I think. I was already working on French and History A Level when I joined the Quarry Men. John and Pete were in 5C I think and Eric in 5B or 5A.

"Following the day I'd bought a banjo. I went to school and told Eric Griffiths that I had just got a banjo and he asked me if I wanted to be in a group with himself, Lennon, Shotton and Bill Smith. I, of course, agreed. He knew I couldn't play it as I had only got it the previous day. When we practised he would shout the chord name at me and very soon I could play by ear. I later bought a banjo tutor and learnt some chord inversions further up the neck, but John insisted I played the same ones as him and Eric.

"The only girlfriend of John's I remember was Barbara Baker as she was also a member of St Peter's Sunday School, but apart from vaguely knowing what she looked like, I remember nothing more about her or John's attitude to girls.

"As for being a 'purist' — I simply didn't like rock and roll very much. I preferred skiffle and trad jazz. I argued with John on stage at the Cavern over his choice of rock rather than skiffle as I was concerned at the audience reaction to our playing rock in a jazz cellar. As soon as I left the Quarry Men I bought a guitar and got into folk music. As I stayed on at Quarry I became part of a jazz trio with a pianist called Gerald Greenwood and a drummer, Les Brough, both from Quarry. We appeared at the Prefects' Rag Concert under the name the Elastic Band."

Shotton says John named the group the Quarry Men because of the school song, which contained the words "Quarry Men, strong before our birth, straining each muscle and sinew."

Lonnie Donegan was their inspiration and they began with a repertoire of skiffle songs such as 'Rock Island Line', 'Puttin On The Style,' 'Cumberland Gap', and 'Maggie May'. They were soon also including Elvis Presley numbers such as 'Blue Moon Of Kentucky,' 'All Shook Up,' 'I'm Left, You're Right, She's Gone' and 'Baby Let's Play House' in addition to numbers such as 'Come Go With Me.'

There was only one microphone and, as it was John's group, he was the one who got it. The group learned the words to songs by listening to them on the radio and scribbling down the words, or going into a record booth and writing out the words until they got thrown out of the record store.

Using this method often resulted in wrong words being used. Commenting on this system of learning songs, Davis said, "John would fill in the missing words and that's how we got the bit about the penitentiary in 'Come Go With Me,' which scanned and fitted in with the themes of skiffle songs. I remember his rewriting 'Streamline Train' as 'Long Black Train,' but he didn't make lyrics up on the hoof."

The group initially played at friend's parties, in skiffle contests and when Nigel was appointed manager by John, he arranged their gig at Lee Park Golf Club which led to their first Cavern booking on 7 August 1957.

Nigel also confirms that the name was always split into two words: Quarry Men and not as later writers put it, as one word: Quarrymen (the group's business card, drums and local adverts at the time, as well as the photograph at the Village Fete clearly show Quarry Men as two words).

The group appeared at the Empire Theatre, Liverpool on Sunday 9 June 1957 in the heat of a talent show called 'TV Star Search' by Carroll Levis, but were unsuccessful. Later that same month they appeared at a street party in Roseberry Street. This took place on Saturday June 22 and came by way of Colin Hanton's friend Charles Roberts, whose mother Marjorie organised the event.

The group performed on the back of a lorry and later had to flee into the Roberts' house when some thugs threatened to beat them up — and they were specifically threatening to John.

Their most important date took place at Woolton Parish Church garden fête on Saturday, July 6 1957 when Ivan Vaughan brought Paul McCartney along to meet John. Although Paul McCartney had been asked to join the group, when they made their Cavern debut on Wednesday 7 August, Paul was away at camp.

The Cavern at this time was strictly a jazz club and skiffle groups were often booked as support acts on the understanding that rock 'n' roll was banned. However, following a performance of 'Come Go With Me',
John decided to introduce some Elvis Presley numbers and performed 'Hound Dog' and 'Blue Suede Shoes', which upset club owner Alan Sytner who sent the Quarry Men a note on stage stating "Cut out the bloody rock!"

"THIS WAS TO BE THE FIRST TIME THAT JOHN AND PAUL APPEARED ON STAGE TOGETHER, WITH PAUL PLAYING A ZENITH GUITAR."

At a Quarry Men booking at New Clubmoor Hall on Friday October 18, Paul McCartney made his debut with the band. They comprised John on rhythm guitar, Len Garry on tea chest bass, Eric Griffiths on guitar, Colin Hanton on drums – and since the venue had a piano, they invited John 'Duff' Lowe to join them (Pete Shotton and Rod Davis had left the group by this time).

Their manager Nigel Walley had arranged the booking. Nigel had suggested that they all wear large check shirts to project a Country and Western image, while John and Paul were to wear white coats.

This was to be the first time that John and Paul appeared on stage together, with Paul playing a Zenith guitar and singing on numbers such as 'Twenty Flight Rock', 'Long Tall Sally' and 'Be Bop A Lula'. Paul was due to play a guitar solo called 'Guitar Boogie'.

This would have been difficult for him as, being left-handed, he'd had to string his instrument for a left-handed player, but the plectrum guard remained affixed above the 6th string, which caused problems. Halfway through playing the instrumental, Paul began to make mistakes and John brought the number to a halt, saying "He's our new boy. He'll be alright given time."
A series of gigs at Wilson Hall in Garston followed, a venue run by popular promoter Charlie McBain, who also booked the group at New Clubmoor Hall.

Paul's second gig with the Quarry Men took place at Wilson Hall, Garston on Thursday November 7 1957. On November 16 they appeared at the Stanley Abattoir Social Club and returned to New Clubmoor Hall on Saturday 23 November.

Another Saturday evening booking at Wilson Hall followed on December 7. The group began their performance with Paul singing 'Twenty Flight Rock' and John followed with 'That'll Be the Day'.

Their first session went well and Paul was able to cope on his 'Guitar Boogie' solo. Their second set went well and they were ready to leave, although they were apprehensive that two local toughs Rodney Johnson and George Wilson might be seeking them out.

They all left to catch buses to their individual destinations and John and Paul went together, carrying the tea chest bass. They were heading towards the bus stop when they noticed Johnson and Wilson, so they left the tea chest in the road and jumped on a bus. To their horror they found that the two toughs had also run after the bus and caught it at the next stop. They were mainly after John, but came on the top deck and began to hit Pete.

John ran downstairs and the two lads ran after him and jumped off the bus. Pete went down expecting to see John battling with them on the pavement, but John had hidden himself away on the lower deck and escaped their attention. The tea chest bass had remained at the side of the road for days and became weather-beaten, but Ivan Vaughan and Len retrieved it and Ivan repaired it.

The Quarry Men began 1958 with a further appearance at New Clubmoor Hall on Friday 10 January. They followed with one further gig that month, a return to the Cavern Club on Friday 24 January.

On Thursday 6 February they appeared at Wilson Hall, where George Harrison, then 14-years-old, was invited along to watch them. Thursday March 13 saw the opening of the Morgue, a tiny cellar club in Broadgreen, run by Alan Caldwell, later to become the legendary Rory Storm.

This was the night it was said that George played 'Raunchy' for them, a brief audition which resulted in him joining the band. They were to make a couple of appearances at the venue. Their final date of the year came through George as they were booked to appear at the wedding reception for George's brother Harry and his bride Irene McCann and performed at the Harrison household at 25 Upton Green, Speke on Saturday 20 December.

During the summer of 1958 they made a record at a small recording studio situated at 53 Kensington in Liverpool, run by Percy Phillips.

Johnny Guitar and Paul Murphy of Rory's Storm's band had gone there earlier to record the number 'Butterfly.' John, Paul, George, John Lowe and Colin Hanton were the Quarry Men appearing at the session during which they recorded two numbers, 'That'll Be The Day,' the Buddy Holly number, with John on lead vocal and 'In Spite Of All The Danger,' a number penned by Paul and George, and credited as such, although Paul was later to state that it was really his composition. They clubbed together to buy a single two-sided shellac disc and Phillips wiped the tape over afterwards.

That one copy ended up in the hands of Lowe, who kept it for decades. Paul bought it from Lowe in 1981 and commented, "It says on the label that it was me and George but I think it was written by me, and George played the guitar solo. It was my song. It's very similar to an Elvis song.

"I remember we went down on the bus with our instruments and waited in the little room outside while somebody else made their demo, and then it was our turn. We just went into the room, hardly saw the engineer because he was next door in a control booth. We ran through it very quickly and it was all over.
"John did 'That'll Be The Day,' which was one of our stage numbers. George played the opening guitar notes and I harmonised with John singing lead."

Their first gig of the New Year was also via the Harrison's with the Quarry Men being booked at Wilson Hall on Thursday January 1 1959 by George's father Harry for a party in aid of the Speke Bus Depot Social Club. The Bus Depot party was supposed to lead to a series of gigs at the Pavilion Theatre as Mr Harrison had talked the manager of the theatre into coming along to listen to them. They got drunk in the interval, had a disastrous show in the second-half and blew their chances of appearing at the Pavilion. After an argument on the bus home, a frustrated Colin Hanton left the group, never to return.

The Quarry Men appeared at Woolton Village Club in Allerton Road on Saturday January 24 1959 and no other official dates are listed for the band until the end of August of that year. It appears that the Quarry Men had actually disbanded, the members going their own ways.

George Harrison was to join another group, the Les Stewart Quartet, who had a residency at Lowlands Club in the West Derby area of Liverpool, while John and Paul met, usually at Paul's house in Forthlin Road, to write songs together.

It was a stroke of luck that revived the group. The Les Stewart Quartet was offered a residency at a new West Derby club, the Casbah, due to open on Saturday August 29 1959. Leader Stewart, irked that guitarist Ken Brown had been missing rehearsals to help with the decoration of the new club, suddenly decided not to accept the residency.

Brown and George left the group and George asked Mrs Mona Best, who was running the Casbah, if they could have the Saturday evening residency if he brought along two of his musician mates. She agreed. George contacted John and Paul and a new four-piece Quarry Men made their debut at the Casbah on Saturday 29 August.

They continued with their Saturday evening appearances until October 10 when Brown couldn't perform with them due to some illness, but still received part of their appearance fee. They argued with Mrs Best, abandoned their residency and ejected Brown.

As a trio they changed their name to Johnny & the Moondogs for some appearances at the Empire Theatre in yet another Carroll Levis talent competition, passed a heat and appeared at the Hippodrome Theatre, Manchester on Sunday November 15, although they had to leave before the end of the show to catch their last train to Liverpool.

Stuart Sutcliffe joined the group in January 1960.

They were now a quartet comprising John, Paul, George and Stuart, sans drummer. They appeared at a number of Art College dances on Saturday evenings, supporting jazz bands such as the Merseysippi, but began to experiment with a number of different names, including the Beatals, the Silver Beats, the Silver Beetles, the Silver Beatles and, finally, the Beatles.

The Quarry Men, as a name, no longer existed.

Thirty-seven years after the original formation, two original members of the Quarry Men, John Lowe and Rod Davis teamed up in 1993 and funded the album "Open for Engagements," which was released on August 1 1994 on Kewbank Records KBCD 111.

They were billed as The Quarry Men featuring John 'Duff' Lowe and Rod Davis. The other members were John Ozoroff on lead guitar and vocals, Charles Hart on drums and Ritchie Gould on bass.

In January 1997, when the new Cavern club celebrated the 40th birthday of the opening of the original club, the former members of the Quarry Men were all invited, together with John Lowe. In evening they were persuaded to perform four numbers with Lennon look-alike Gary Gibson.

Rod Davis commented: "I hadn't been in touch with the others for 40 years. We hadn't been invited to play. I just went along for the free drink, but I put an old tea chest and washboard in the boot of my car, just in case. In the event, we did play together for the first time in four decades."

This led to their appearance at the 40th anniversary of the St Peter's Church Hall fete on Saturday 5 July 1997. The original Rose Queen Sally Wright was in attendance to crown the present Rose Queen and the original lorry driver Doug Chadwick drove the Quarry Men around.

The personnel comprised Pete Shotton on washboard, Colin Hanton on drums, Eric Griffiths on guitar, Len Garry on tea chest bass and Rod Davis on banjo. John Lowe was there but they wouldn't let him play because they said he was a Quarry Man at a later date. The group performed 'Rock Island Line,' 'Maggie May,' 'Cumberland Gap,' 'Baby Let's Play House,' 'Twenty Flight Rock,' 'Come Go With Me' and 'Worried Man Blues.'

The occasion saw messages of good will from Yoko Ono, Cynthia Lennon, George Martin, Tony Blair, the Queen and Paul McCartney. 3000 people attended the event. Pete Shotton sang 'Imagine' in the evening at the church Hall and it was the first time he'd ever sung solo.

The show was recorded and issued on a 15 track CD in mid-November 1997 under the title 'John Lennon's Original Quarry Men Get Back Together.'

Another important Quarry Bank schoolmate was Mike Hill. Mike has lived in Australia for many years. He lived at 69 Dovedale Road until he was 22 and then went to work abroad.

He was to tell me: "My house was at the other end of Dovedale Road from Dovedale Road School and from Penny Lane. I was near the Rose Lane end of Dovedale Road. I first met John after he moved in to live with his Aunt Mimi.

He joined Dovedale Road Infants School when he was five. We were in the same class in primary and junior schools, both passed our 11-plus exam and both went on together to Quarry Bank where I first met Pete Shotton. John and Pete were inseparable at QB and they, together with me and my friend Don Beatty, made a frequent foursome.

"Don, Pete and I went on a Liverpool grammar school's exchange holiday in Amsterdam in April 1956 when we were all aged 15. John didn't come.

"We had a ball. I returned with Little Richard's record of 'Long Tall Sally' with 'Slippin' an' Slidin'' on the B side. At that time we used to regularly break school rules and cycle to my house from QB on school days at lunch time.

"Just after the Amsterdam trip on one of those lunchtime sessions I played John the record having first got his attention by telling him the singer was better than Elvis Presley. Well, it stopped John in his tracks and he was lost for words. This was so unusual we all remembered it.

"When Pete Shotton's book came out after John's murder, he described this incident in detail as it was in every sense a critical moment in John's life.

"I was also a close school friend of John's for 12 years from when we were five until we were almost 17 and we both left Quarry Bank in July 1957."

The Beatles, Little Richard, Joe Ankrah, Sugar Dean and Derry Wilkie

Bill Harry

St Peter's Church, Woolton
Left: Ivan Vaughan, who introduced
John Lennon and Paul McCartney

Ged Fleming

ST. PETER'S CHURCH FIELD

Situated in Church Road, Woolton, Liverpool L25, the grounds provided the site of the historic occasion on Saturday 6 July 1957 when John Lennon and Paul McCartney met for the first time.

The event was the annual summer fête and Pete Shotton's mum had secured a booking at the event for the Quarry Men.

At 2pm, five flatbed lorries set out from Church Road, with the Quarry Men aboard the last one, a coal lorry. On another truck, sitting in a chair under a flower-bedecked trellis was thirteen-year-old Sally Wright, the Rose Queen, dressed in a white lace gown with a train of pink velvet. The 25-man Band of the Cheshire Yeomanry led the procession as it entered Allerton Road, then

John Lennon with the Quarry Men in 1957

Woolton Street, Kings Drive, Hunt's Cross Avenue and back to Church Road. Accompanying the procession on foot were Girl Guides and Brownies, Boy Scouts and Cubs and Morris Dancers. Shortly before 3 pm they arrived at St Peter's church field and the procession ended, while the Yeomanry Band entered the field and continued to entertain the crowd. The Quarry Men stored their equipment in the Scouts Hut and began to wander round the various stalls. After the crowning of the Rose Queen, there was a Fancy Dress competition. At 4.15pm the Quarry Men lugged their equipment onto the stage, which was slightly under three feet high and was 25 feet wide by 15 feet deep.

The Quarry Men that day featured John Lennon, Eric Griffiths, Colin Hanton, Rod Davis, Pete Shotton and Len Garry while Geoff Rhind, a schoolboy with a Box Brownie, took photographs of them for posterity. Geoff, who now lives in Ireland, recalled that

the music was 'extremely loud,' and took the famous pictures with his new black plastic Kodak Comer camera.

On the historic day that John met Paul, Mimi couldn't find John. So she went along to the fête by herself where she met some of her sisters and other members of the family. It wasn't until John actually went on stage that she knew he was even taking part in the fete.

She was to say, "I was having a cup of tea in the refreshment tent. Suddenly, in the midst of everything, came this . . . this eruption of noise. Everyone had drained away from were I stood, in the field next door. And there on the stage I saw them, John and that Shotton.

"John saw me standing there with my mouth open. He started to

47

IN THIS HALL ON
6TH JULY 1957
JOHN & PAUL
FIRST MET

The Quarry Men featuring, Eric Griffiths,
Colin Hanton, Rod Davies, John Lennon,
Pete Shotton and Len Garry performed on
the afternoon of 6th July 1957 at St Peters
Church Fete. In the evening before their
performance in this hall Ivan Vaughan,
who sometimes played in the group,
introduced his friend Paul McCartney to
John Lennon. As John recalled ......

" that was the day, the day
that I met Paul, that it
started moving. "

PAUL McCARTNEY

JOHN LENNON

make words up about me in the song he was singing. 'Mimi's coming down the path' he sang."

Another member of the audience also found his attendance at the event was to bring him a small fortune in later years. He was 16-year-old Bob Molyneux, a member, along with John, of St Peter's Youth club. Bob was an amateur recording enthusiast and had brought along his portable Grundig reel-to-reel tape recorder.

He commented, "Half the music at the dance was the George Edwards Band. They were an old-fashioned dance group, doing quicksteps and foxtrots and waltzes. Useless really. The youngsters wanted to get jiving, you see. The Quarry Men were very well received.

"There was no special lighting, so it was very dim in there. My first priority was just to get plugged in to the nearest power socket, which was in an adjoining room, so I had to run an extension lead through.

"I had this Grundig TKB tape-recorder, heavy, but just about portable. It had cost me 82 guineas, which was a lot of money then, so very few 16-year-olds had anything like it.

"I didn't have to get any permission, just walked in and did it. I don't think they even noticed me, it was so dark. I had to keep my leads near the wall so the dancers wouldn't trip over it. I positioned myself about fifteen yards back from the stage, and held the mike up in my hand. I got them doing 'Baby Let's Play House,' which was an Elvis Presley thing, and 'Puttin' on the Style,' which was the Lonnie Donegan hit.

He listened to the Quarry Men and was not impressed, saying that their music was "pretty run-of-the-mill."

Molyneux was also to comment, "John didn't move when he was singing but during the instrumental break he'd dance about and sing in a screechy type voice. You could see he was the leader. He had a very commanding voice."

Years later he spotted Ringo Starr in a Liverpool club and told him about the tapes, saying John could have them. However, he didn't hear anything back and forgot about the tapes until he came across them again in 1994 and put them up for auction at

Sotheby's. EMI bought them for £78,500.
Molyneux became a policeman, now retired, and he and his wife Sarah and daughter Kate live near Southampton.

As Ivan Vaughan, John's close childhood friend, wasn't playing tea-chest bass that day he invited his Liverpool Institute friend Paul McCartney. Ivan felt that Paul should meet John and invited him along to see the Quarry Men at the fete – with the enticement that it was a good place to meet girls. He was to say of Paul, "I knew this was a great fellow. I only ever brought along great fellows to meet John."

They had been playing for about ten minutes when Paul McCartney arrived on his bike, his guitar strapped to his back. Hoping to pick up a girl, he was dressed in a white sports jacket and black drainpipe trousers. He spotted Ivan Vaughan and they went up to listen to the Quarry Men as they played 'Come Go With Me,' which had been a hit for the Dell Vikings. John didn't know all the words to the song, but made some of them up, which he did quite often. They finished playing at around 5pm and made way for the military band, which were followed by the Police dog display. Shortly after 6pm the Quarry Men took to the stage again, the last outdoor performance of the day.

During the Quarry Men's performance they played 'Baby Let's Play House', 'Maggie May', 'Cumberland Gap', 'Railroad Bill', 'Putting On the Style' and 'Come Go With Me'.

After they'd finished playing and took their gear over to the church hall where they were performing that evening, Ivan took the fifteen-year-old Paul across to meet them.

The young lad made an impression because he showed them how to tune a guitar, which none of the band could do. He particularly impressed John with his knowledge of the lyrics of rock 'n' roll songs and even wrote out the words of 'Twenty Flight Rock' and 'Be-Bop-A-Lula' for John. To cap it all, he borrowed a guitar and began to play some Little Richard numbers, including 'Long Tall Sally' and 'Tutti Frutti'.

Paul McCartney was to tell Record Collector magazine: "I remember coming into the fête and seeing all the sideshows, and also hearing all this great music wafting in from this little Tannoy system. It was John and the band. I remember I was amazed and

John with Nigel Walley, manager of the Quarry Men

Nigel Walley

thought, 'Oh great', because I was obviously into the music. I remember John singing a song called 'Come Go With Me.' He'd heard it on the radio. He didn't really know the verses, but he knew the chorus. The rest he just made up himself. I just thought, 'Well, he looks good, he's singing well and he seems like a great lead singer to me.' Of course, he had his glasses off, so he really looked suave. I remember John was good. He was really the only outstanding member, all the rest kind of slipped away."

A local newspaper reported: "An entirely different type of music was provided by the Quarry Men Skiffle Group. These five boys are members of the youth club and some of them are pupils of Quarry Bank High School. Recently they appeared in the Carroll Levis Discoveries show at a Liverpool theatre, but unfortunately did not quite qualify for the finals. They are John Lennon, who plays the guitar and is the popular vocalist, Peter Shotton (washboard), Eric Griffiths (guitar), Len Garry (bass) and Rodney Davis (banjo). Colin Hanton, who is the drummer, did not appear on Saturday. Their songs included 'Cumberland Gap', 'Maggie May' and 'Railroad Bill'.

John enters
Liverpool
College of Art

The Dissenters
vow to make
Liverpool famous

John meets
Cynthia Powell

John moves into
Gambier
Terrace

CHAPTER 4
DESIGNS FOR LIFE

LIVERPOOL COLLEGE OF ART

Situated in Hope Street – an appropriate name for the street that has a cathedral at each end.

John entered the Art College at the age of 16 in September 1957. He started life at the school, dressed in Teddy boy gear, and began the Intermediate course. This was a course in which all the basics were taught: composition, life drawing and so on. Among the friends John made in his class were Geoff Mohammed, Tony Carricker, Ann Mason and Helen Anderson. One of his first girlfriends at the college was Thelma Pickles. Other members of his Intermediate class included Carol Balfour, Jeff Cane, John Wild, Peter Williams, Gill Taylor, Marcia Coleman, Ann Preece, Violet Upton, Diane Molyneux, Ann Curtis and Sheila Jones. Ann Mason was to spend two hours painting a picture of John in March 1958.

John gained a reputation for disrupting classes and was turned down for the painting class. Whilst the Intermediate course continued, in place of the painting class he took lettering, in which there were approximately a dozen students in the class including Cynthia Powell, Phyllis McKenzie and Jonathan Hague. Cynthia had joined the lettering class in her second year at the college.

John mixed with various groups of friends in the college. After I'd introduced him to Stuart Sutcliffe and Rod Murray at Ye Cracke in Rice Street, the college watering hole, we were often mixing together socially at parties and local pubs, at coffee bars such as the Jacaranda and in students flats. First Rod and Stuart had accommodation in nearby Percy Street and then they moved to Gambier Terrace, where lots of gatherings between them took place.

The four of us also used to go to the nearby Liverpool University where subsidised drinks could be had at the student's bar and we

Liverpool College of Art on Hope Street

went to various university events, such as poetry readings and also took part in the annual Panto Day. This was an event for local charities in which the university students collected money in tins and also had floats on the backs of lorries, which paraded in the city centre. Some members of the Art College participated as well as members of Liverpool Institute such as Paul McCartney and George Harrison. John was known to go to the toilets in Lime Street station where, inside a closet, he'd jimmy open his collection box and spend the money on beer!

Ye Cracke is where Stuart Sutcliffe's father often dropped in to have a drink with Arthur Ballard, one of the tutors, who was a great help to us and who actually prevented John and me from being expelled. Arthur attempted to get both of us into the new graphic arts department. I was accepted but the teacher Roy Sharp rejected John because of his reputation for disruptive behaviour. Another pub we frequented was the Philharmonic, on Hope Street.

John was always having a laugh in classes, particularly when a teacher was out of the room – and often got up to high jinks in the life classes, sitting in the lap of nude model June Furlong, for example. June celebrated her 80th birthday in May 2010 and had been a celebrated model in London in her youth, posing for the major painters of the day, before returning to Liverpool to settle in her family home.

Posing in the nude in front of a large class is usually a serious business, but John often caused chaos for June, who remembers one incident in which he jumped from behind his easel as soon as the teacher left the room and sat on her knee and began groping her and necking with her. On another occasion he handed teacher Terry Griffiths his drawing of June in the nude, which consisted solely of a sketch of her wristwatch. June lent John some of her clothing when he appeared in an Art College pantomime of 'Cinderella' in 1959. John was an ugly sister, together with his mate

Geoff Mohammed and the clothes June lent him included a pair of pink corsets, a dark blue dress with white polka dot decoration, a straw hat with pink and blue feather decoration and a pair of Victorian pinchback earrings.

June put all of the items up for auction at the Eldon E Worrall sale in Liverpool in 1985. As for the pantomime itself – towards the end of 1959 John, Stuart and Rod Murray began writing a satirical pantomime about 'Cinderella' at the flat in 9 Percy Street, which they performed at the Art College soon after.

The characters included two ugly sisters Hortense (Hort) and Gwyneth (Gwyn) played by John and his mate Geoff Mohammed. Ella (Cinders) was played by June Harry, Fairy Snow, the Fairy Godmother was played by Stuart Sutcliffe, Boris (Dandienne) was played by Rod Murray and Fred (Prince Charming) was played by John Chase.

John's hand can clearly be found in the script with his references to cripples and his nonsense Lewis Carrol-esque wordplay.

An example is the dream sequence with the ugly sisters, called 'Ballet Dream':
John: "You brackish swine, thou pie swab fit."
Geoff: "Help us gayn to woothy grit."
John: "Go hence thee battered bun of bane."
Geoff: "File on you crut, so there a pain."
John: "Don't quote my wrath please, Kipper head."
In the meantime, throughout the pantomime, Ella keeps repeating "I got a painting in the John Moores Show."
Buttons: "Ah, poor girl: I must go and console her. So you have a painting in the John Moores? How marvellous!"
Ella: "But Hort and Gwyneth won't let me go to the private view."
Buttons: "Perhaps it's for the best. They are terrible things."
Ella: "But I wanted to be terribly arty and make people think I'm a beatnikker."
Buttons: "Poor darling."

Incidentally, it was while they were writing this very pantomime in the Percy Street flat that John offered Stuart and Rod the opportunity of playing bass guitar with his group.
The Student's Union organised dances in the college canteen, and mainly booking local jazz bands such as the Merseysippi. Stuart and I were among the organisers, with me designing the tickets and

Ged Fleming

The Philharmonic, a favourite haunt for the Liverpool College of Art students

collecting them at the door. We obviously booked John's group, referred to as the college band. With Stuart and me on the student's union committee were Rod Murray, Alan Swerdlow and Rod Jones, who were also their friends. Alan was commissioned by Brian Epstein to take photographs of the Beatles at the Odd Spot club and to design a Beatles Fan Club night ticket and Mersey Beat advert.

Rod Jones shared the Gambier Terrace flat with Stuart and Rod – where John virtually moved in, although initially he wasn't strictly an official tenant. Since they were booked at the college dances they asked Stuart and me if we could get them some PA equipment and Stuart and I proposed and seconded that the union pay for amplification equipment, which 'the college band' could use. They never returned it and its loss was thought to be the reason why Stuart was rejected for the ATD (Art Teachers Training) course.

John's fashions changed from the early days he was at the college. His initial Teddy boy style of dress is what first drew my attention to him. I noticed him striding past in the canteen in his Teddy boy gear and observed that all the other students were dressed in turtle neck sweaters and duffle coats – making John the 'outsider' or the unconventional one. He later began to adopt a more bohemian style although he was never to actually conform.

"JOHN AND I HAD A REBELLIOUS STREAK, SO IT WAS AWFUL. WE COULDN'T WAIT TO GROW UP AND TELL EVERYONE TO GET LOST."

As Paul and George were in the building next door, they frequently came into the college canteen at lunchtimes and also used to rehearse in the college life rooms during breaks.

Stuart's best friend was Rod Murray, from the West Derby area, who enrolled at the college in 1958. They rented no less than three different flats together, ending up in Gambier Terrace where John began staying on a regular basis. It was Rod who joined John, Stuart and me in the Dissenters and when John needed a bass guitarist for his group, he offered the job to both Rod and Stu. Rod began to make a bass guitar, but Stu sold a painting and was able to buy a guitar on hire purchase, and thus became a Beatle instead of Rod. Shortly before John began his affair with Cynthia, he had been dating 16-year-old art student Thelma Pickles, who had been introduced to him by another student, Helen Anderson.

He called her 'Thel' and they were "going steady" for six months before the romance just fizzled out. They were both rebels in the way they dressed and had several things in common; including the fact that Thelma's father had deserted her when she was a child. She was able to stand up to him during John's moods, which he appreciated, and at one time in Ye Cracke pub when he began shouting at her, she told him "Don't take it out on me just because your mother's dead!"

Describing how she and John felt when they were sixteen, she said: "We were always being told what we couldn't do. He and I had a rebellious streak, so it was awful. We couldn't wait to grow up and tell everyone to get lost. Mimi hated his tight trousers and my mother hated my black stockings. It was a horrible time to be young!"

She was also to say, "John had a complete disrespect for everything, but he always had an audience around him."
Thelma was dated by Paul McCartney for a while and eventually married Roger McGough, one of Liverpool's premier poets, who was also a member of the popular and successful trio the Scaffold. They were later divorced, Thelma left Liverpool and moved to London to enjoy a successful career in television and was one of the producers of Cilla Black's 'Blind Date' series at London Weekend Television. She later moved to New Zealand.

John also fancied Jonni Crosby, a Brigitte Bardot look-alike. Another student was Helen Anderson who had also attended the Liverpool School of Art in Gambier Terrace when Cynthia Powell and I were students. I must admit I was envious of her talent — she was an amazing girl who was destined to find success in whatever she wanted to do.

Helen had received publicity in the press because she'd painted a portrait of Lonnie Donegan and she and John became close friends, although the relationship was platonic. He also called her 'Heloon.' Cynthia was jealous and realized she loved John when she noticed Helen stroking his hair one day.

During the first year at college John fancied a baggy bright yellow cable knit sweater Helen was wearing and asked if she'd give it to him. Helen was to say: "I started off in the same class as John at Liverpool Art College in 1958. Somebody knitted the jumper for me and John coveted it. I said I'd swap it for one of his drawings and he gave me the book and said, 'Here, take the lot'.

"I have looked at them often over the years and they always make me laugh."

The book was actually an exercise book from his Quarry Bank days with 22 caricatures of teachers and fellow pupils.

Typical Hairy Hairless Smell-Type Smith was Bill Smith, a classmate who was one of the first people recruited for John's skiffle group the Quarry Men. His Hairy Hairless Highness Dr Mick Fishwick was another fellow student, John Morris. Nick O'Teen, Irish Madman was the Quarry Bank Latin master John Colvin and A Simple Soul On The Farm was school groundsman Albert Yoxhall. The caricature of John was labeled simply A Simple Pimple Short-Sighted John Wimple Lennon.

In 1984 Yoko and Sean visited the college and donated £10,000 and a number of John's drawings to it. During the trip Yoko was given a copy of John's college report from 1958-1960 in which he had failed two Intermediate exams. A teacher had written "Give up your guitar, otherwise you will never pass your exams."

Another important friend of John's was Jonathan Hague, who told me: "I was born and brought up in Wales and I think the country bumpkin upbringing helped my relationship with John, him being the tough city lad showing me the city life, teaching me to drink, etc.

"I spent the most time with John when we were both studying Intermediate in our second year. This was a course ending in an examination for the National Diploma in Design. We were split into separate classes for crafts. John and I did lettering, together with Cynthia and a girlfriend of hers called Phyllis (McKenzie).

"John failed his Intermediate because of lettering and at his second sitting he seemed to be beyond caring. I remember feeling very concerned because he was thinking of Hamburg. He once told me he would have finished college, but for Intermediate – and then what would have happened to the Beatles?!"

Jonathan has many memories of the art school days and says, "I remember Arthur Ballard used to take us every Monday morning in a small room where our pictures would be hung on a wall. This was the 'composition' homework and he would give us a big crit on them, discussing each one individually.

"They were the usual subjects for such studies: the railway station, a restaurant, the docks, roadworks, etc. For some reason John would get away with presenting one of his cartoon drawings each week. For instance he would have hundreds of little Dockers climbing over a boat. And his railway station was just a man's foot disappearing down a staircase.

"He was always the entertainer. The atmosphere in the life class when we drew from live models was always like that of a church. Everyone would sit in silence taking their drawing seriously. John would start by making the tiniest noise, then create a snigger which he'd let grow louder, bit by bit, 'til he had the whole room erupting in bursts of laughter. I remember the metalwork teacher took John outside the room into the passageway one day to give him a ticking off because John had cut out some monster-type figure.

"I heard the teacher saying, 'what do you think you will end up doing?' 'I want to be a pop star.'

"The teacher groaned and said, 'Be realistic!' ".

Jonathan attained his ATD (Art Teachers Diploma). He says, "After ATD I obtained a British Council scholarship to the Hague for about 18 months, but stayed for three years. I took the scholarship as my last chance and worked every day – and with luck held a number of private gallery exhibitions there, one at the Gemeentee Museum itself. I sent John a catalogue."

Jonathan received a letter from John, thanking him for his note:

"So there you are in Holland with all those clogs, eh? Glad you are now a FAMOUS PAINTER – just like Arthur Ballard said you would be! The catalogue looked great, seems you've forgotten all about Bratby! I still can't paint – but still do, if you see what I mean, ANYWAY – I'm pleased to hear from you. My address is not so special – but here it is.

> J Lennon
> Kenwood, St George's Hill
> Cavendish Road
> Weybridge
> Surrey

"If you write – try and use a similar type of envelope to the one you sent – you know BROWN – or your letter might get lost in the happy fan mail.
"See or hear you soon.
"Good Heavens.
"John. A band (Lennon)."

Jonathan continued, "After I left Holland, which I've always regretted, I did a two-week teaching job at both Coventry and Birmingham art schools for five years. I had a number of private gallery exhibitions as well, plus paintings in the Royal Academy etc, and started seeing Lennon again, him showing me the Big City again: this time, London."

When Jonathan was 29, John and Paul McCartney sponsored an exhibition of his work. He says: "One day I took my paintings in a huge roll to his house and we spread them all over his sitting room.

"SO THERE YOU ARE IN HOLLAND WITH ALL THOSE CLOGS, EH? GLAD YOU ARE NOW A FAMOUS PAINTER – JUST LIKE ARTHUR BALLARD SAID YOU WOULD BE!"

A portrait of Lennon by his art student friend Jonathon Hague

"He liked them, hence the exhibition. He dragged Paul in on it, but I don't think Paul was very keen, although he didn't mind putting up the money."

The exhibition took place at the Royal Institute Gallery, 195 Piccadilly from 4-23 December, 1967 and there was a diverse selection of paintings whose subjects included the Beatles, Mick Jagger, Vincent Van Gogh and the funeral of Sir Winston Churchill.
Cynthia's best friend was Phyllis McKenzie. Phyllis first knew John when she attended St Peter's, Woolton and her father had lived in a flat in the same house as John's grandparents, the Stanleys. Phyllis was also present at St Peter's fete when John and Paul met for the first time. She also knew John at Liverpool College of Art.

Cynthia Powell first met Phyllis McKenzie at the Junior College of Art in Gambier Terrace.
When they both attended Liverpool College of Art they became the best of friends. There were a number of lessons in the Intermediate Course which students could opt for and Cynthia and Phyl chose to attend the lettering class twice a week. Among the dozen or so students present in the lessons were John and his friend Jonathan Hague.
Phyl accompanied Cynthia when John first invited her to join him for

a drink at Ye Cracke pub. Phyllis had known John since he first enrolled at the college because they both lived in the Woolton area and used to travel on the same bus, the No 72, each morning. They often chatted, with John sometimes offering to pay her fare.

When Cynthia began to stay overnight at Gambier Terrace with John she used to tell her mother that she was staying with Phyllis.

In April 1963, when Cynthia was expecting Julian, Phyllis decided to stay with her until the baby was born. She was woken in the middle of the night when Cynthia yelled out that the baby was imminent and they phoned for an ambulance. Phyllis accompanied Cynthia to Sefton General Hospital dressed only in a nightie, dressing gown and slippers, with her hair in curlers. Once Cynthia was admitted, Phyl was told she couldn't stay and wouldn't be given a lift back home in an ambulance.

Without any money on her person she set off on a long walk of several miles, dressed only in her nightclothes. After she'd travelled about two miles, a taxi driver took pity on her, saying "Hey, love, I don't think it's advisable to walk round the streets of Liverpool at this time of night dressed like that, do you?" and agreed to take her the rest of the way home.

Following Julian's birth, Cynthia initially attempted to keep her identity secret and when people asked her if she was Cynthia Lennon, she denied it and said her name was Phyllis McKenzie.

Cynthia's friendship with Phyllis continued throughout the years and it was Phyllis who introduced Cynthia to her third husband, John Twist. The two women had a joint exhibition of their work in 1999. It took place in June and July at the KDK Gallery in Portobello Road and the exhibition was called 'Lennon and McKenzie', although her married name is Fearon.

There were two sides to John's associations at the college. There was his wild side, which he shared with his mates Tony Carricker, Geoff Mohammed and Jeff Cane and there was his serious and creative side which he shared with Stuart, Rod and me.

Tony was in the same class as John and soon came under his influence. John, Tony and Geoff in particular, caused regular disruption in the corridors of the Art College with their pranks. Geoff was born in Manchester of an Indian father and French/Italian mother, and was to become one of John's closest friends. At a class Christmas party in 1958 Geoff had been trying to interest John in Cynthia, saying, "Cynthia likes you, you know." John danced with her and asked if she'd like to come to a party the next day, but she told him she was engaged to a boy in Hoylake. "I didn't ask you to marry me," he said.

At one time John and Geoff went on a drunken spree and brought a number of the souvenirs they'd pinched into the college canteen, including signposts, posters and street nameplates. Geoff was later expelled from the college and returned to Manchester where, sadly, he died in the Seventies.

Philip Norman in his renowned biography of John says Russell Jeffrey Mohammed was ten years older than John and refers to him throughout as Jeff Ray Coleman, in his biography of John it says he was five years older than John and refers to him as Geoff. I also refer to him as Geoff because this is how people spelt his name at the time – an example is the pantomime written with John, Stuart and Rod in which Geoff teamed up with John as an ugly sister.

Margaret Duxbury was another friend who shared the Gambier Terrace flat with Rod, Stuart, John and Diz. She was known as 'Duckie.'

John Lennon with his wife Cynthia and Paul McCartney in 1968

Her son Ed told me: "Margaret joined the art college a year after John. She shared classes with John and Stuart and said she or Stuart was always top in the class. She excelled at painting and went on to have a great deal of success in the 1970s, 80s and early 90s (as Margaret Chapman) with her paintings of Edwardian street scenes selling in 50 countries around the world. Several of her exhibitions were sell-outs.

"She lived with Stuart, Rod and Diz at 3 Gambier Terrace. John Lennon was invited to stay later when he moved out of his house with Aunt Mimi for a time.

"Margaret recalled the flats having a wooden fire escape up which Paul and George used to climb to get in to rehearse – through the window. She remembered Paul coming in through the window and saying 'Ey up, Duckie' or such.

"She thought young George was lovely, quiet and very good-looking. They would rehearse at the flat. John asked her what the band should be called and she suggested the John Lennon Quartet, which John liked.

"The flatmates broke up all the wooden furniture in the flat and used it as firewood, which not surprisingly upset the landlady when she came round (note: This actually happened at the Percy Street flat, not Gambier Terrace). John, Paul and George all used to cheat at Monopoly to the extent that Margaret would refuse to play the game with them.

"She remembered how John would hang about in the art college corridors, leaning on a wall or radiator with his friend Geoff Mohammed and others and he would always have some snide comment to make. She and her friends hated walking up the stairs past them. Lennon would have some witty put-down which the girls dreaded.

"John, Margaret said, was also always imitating spastics and cripples. He would pull faces of and at them, being particularly cruel. She didn't think much of John's artistic abilities in class, certainly not compared to Stuart.

"The first time she was alone with John was at 3 Gambier Terrace. John was waiting for Stu. He had not moved in at this stage. Margaret was worried, thinking he would be the same acerbic guy, ever ready with a put-down. But, of course he showed a different side. In fact he handed her some writing he had recently completed. It was mainly conversation between John and Aunt Mimi as he came home at night.

> 'That you John?'
> 'No, it's Winston Churchill.'
> 'You all right?'
> 'Yes, go back to bed.'

"That sort of thing. Anyway, it must have been a bit more evocative as Margaret told John it was very good. Did he know the book 'The Catcher In The Rye' that was similar in its use of conversation, where the speaker is not identified, she said?

"John had not read it, nor even heard of it. Margaret lent him her copy (never returned). She maintained that she heard John later say that 'The Catcher In The Rye' was one of his favourite books. Of course, John's killer (another M Chapman) made his own twisted interpretation of the book.

"Like most students, she smoked rolled cigarettes in Ye Cracke."

I have fond memories of Margaret who, I remember at the time, had an intense crush on Rod (Jones or Murray, both of whom shared the flat? Sadly, Rod Jones died in October 2002.) Margaret did tell me she had a crush on Rod Jones, Rod Murray says no, she was his girlfriend – although I thought Rod's girlfriend was Diz. At an all-night party in an artist's flat off Duke Street, she'd had an argument with Rod Jones and was distressed, so I spent the hours until morning talking to her and then walked her to Central Station."

I also remember an occasion when she shared a top floor flat in Huskisson Street with Diz, prior to moving into Gambier Terrace. The main room had a double bed, and in the kitchen there was a record player on which Frank Sinatra's 'Songs for Swinging Lovers' was played and re-played throughout the night.

At one point in the early hours John devised a game and asked us all to sit in a circle on the floor.
One person was to say the first thing that came into his head and the person next to him did the same and so on, round and round the circle, time and time again. John did come out with words such as 'spastics' and 'cripples' and, on reflection, it was a clever sort of game, which in some ways could reveal thoughts in a person's head, which they exposed through the speed and spontaneity of the game.

Margaret had indeed become tired and lay on the bed. When the game finished John noticed she was asleep and in his glee came up with the spider idea. He got a bag of potatoes from the kitchen and picked out a selection, then had us stick matchsticks to them to imitate a spider's legs. Then we tied about half a dozen of them from the ceiling dangling above Margaret's head.

I don't remember what happened later as I fell asleep myself. In those days, at parties, we usually kipped on the floor, or on chairs or settees or whatever. Margaret had four children, Esme, Zoe, Edward and Ivan and became an extremely popular artist. Sadly, she died in July 2000. Margaret was born in Darwen, Lancashire and for the last 14 years of her life lived in Southport.

Finally I must mention David Little. David still maintains all his drawings of students and teachers from his time at the college, including his sketches of John, Stuart and myself. Dave now lives in France. The college itself was sold to a building company who intend to turn it into apartments.

YE CRACKE

This is a public house in Rice Street, Liverpool L1. It was the nearest pub to the Liverpool College of Art. When we were students it became our local watering hole.

It has its significance in the romance between John and his future wife Cynthia.

Following a college party in which John asked for a dance with Cynthia, he invited Cynthia to Ye Cracke for a drink and later that evening he took her to the Gambier Terrace flat and they made love for the first time.

Arthur Ballard, one of the college lecturers, used to tutor some of his pupils in the War Office, a tiny room in the pub, so named because it was where regulars used to discuss the events of the Crimean War, as they occurred. He also met Stuart Sutcliffe's father here on a number of occasions.

Once when they were standing outside the pub at lunchtime, drinks in hand, John and Cynthia spotted actor John Gregson (a Liverpool-born British film star whose most popular film was 'Genevieve'). John desperately looked around for something unusual for the actor to sign. He spotted an old boot and asked Gregson to autograph it. The actor was amused by the gesture and signed it across the stitching.

Painter Adrian Henri remembered one incident at Ye Cracke where John was lying on the floor miming swimming movements. A barmaid told him to stop and he said, "I can't stop, or I'll drown!"

John and Stuart Sutcliffe also used to discuss art and artists, with Stu filling John in with the background to art movements of the early 20th century such as the Dada School.

John and I also used to have long conversations together in our favourite seat, beneath an etching of 'The Death Of Nelson'. This was a monochrome version of a huge painting at the Walker Art Gallery. It depicts a dying Admiral Nelson in Hardy's arms, with the sailors on both sides turning away from the duo. John always referred to it as 'Who farted?'

I once told John that I'd heard he wrote poetry and asked if I could

Ye Cracke

Bill Harry

see some. At first embarrassed, because he liked to maintain his macho image, John then produced a sample.

It was a piece of rustic wit, which I found both amusing and charming. I was particularly pleased to note it was in the English tradition of comic humour, in contrast to the Beat poetry of San Francisco that so many British poets were copying. I remembered this when I commissioned John to write a piece about the origin of the Beatles for Mersey Beat.

Although I was aware of John's influences, ranging from Stanley Unwin with his 'Fractured English' to the Goons, this particular poem pre-dated similar stuff many years later from Benny Hill!

Owl George ee be a farmer's lad
With mucklekak and cow
Ee be the son of 'is owl Dad
But why I don't know how

Ee tak a fork and bale the hay
And stacking-stook he stock
And lived his loif from day to day
Dressed in a sweaty sock

One day maybe he marry be
To Nellie Nack the Lass
And we shall see what we shall see
A-fucking in the grass

Our Nellie be a gal so fine
All dimpled wart and blue
She herds the pigs, the rotten swine
It mak me wanna spew!

Somehaps perchance ee'll be a man
But now I will unfurl
Owl George is out of the frying pan
'Cos ee's a little girl

The Dissenters'
plaque in Ye Cracke

On Friday 24 June and Saturday 25 June, 1960 the Beat poet Royston Ellis (advertised as 'Britain's foremost exponent of 'Beat Poetry') held a lecture 'Jazz and Poetry' in the basement coffee bar at Liverpool University during an Arts Festival.

After attending his lecture, during which Royston read some of his poems, John Lennon, Stuart Sutcliffe, Rod Murray and I retired to Ye Cracke to discuss it. I pointed out that we had an undue amount of cultural input from America – with American music, films, books, poetry and even comics being generally looked upon as more glamorous than the British creative arts.

A big influence at the moment was Jack Kerouac, the Beat poets and the American Beat generation, which had led to a section of British youth becoming 'Beatniks.' Yet John's poems, for instance, weren't copies of the American Beat poets, but had a particular 'Englishness' to them.

We began to talk about Liverpool 8 and the talent in the area, artists such as Arthur Dooley and Sam Walsh, writers, art students, even the range of characters we met in pubs with their ready Scouse wit and tremendous sense of humour.

The main point we focussed on was the fact that creative people should draw inspiration from the environment around them and not from environments elsewhere which they had no experience of. Why try to copy the style of American writers and poets who were writing about their own surroundings and experience, when we had our own exciting city to inspire us?

Then and there we took a view that we would use our creative efforts to make Liverpool famous. We then vowed that John would do it with his music, Stuart and Rod with their painting and me with my writing. We also decided on a name for our little group – 'The Dissenters.'

John succeeded beyond all expectations with his music; Stuart would have become a world-class painter if he had lived, Rod became a prominent tutor at a major London art college and I created the phrase Mersey Beat and launched the newspaper of that name. So in no small way, the Dissenters honoured their vow!

THE WALKER ART GALLERY.

Between 17 November 1959 and 17 January 1960, the second bicentennial of the John Moores Exhibition took place at the Walker Art Gallery.

Among the judges were Cornish artist Peter Lanyon and John Moores himself. There were over 2,000 entries from around the country, including one from Arthur Ballard, our favourite tutor at the art college. Stuart also decided to enter the competition and opted to submit his large 'Summer Painting', which was actually in two parts, each measuring six feet by four feet.

His best friend Rod Murray, who helped to carry the painting down to the Walker with Stu, described it as "A great big abstract expressionist painting with sand and lots of wax and stuff to build it up."

When the two returned to their Gambier Terrace flat they decided not to bother taking the other half of the painting. Stu attended the formal exhibition dinner with his girlfriend Susan Williams and was duly delighted when John Moore's himself paid £65 for the work.

The association with John revolved around the fact that John had invited both Rod and John to become bass guitarist with his group. Neither of them had enough money to invest in purchasing a guitar, even on hire purchase. As a result, Rod started to actually build a guitar, but with his good fortune Stuart was able to go down to Hessy's and pick out a guitar he noticed in the window. He placed a deposit on the guitar – not using the money to buy it outright as people have previously written – and became a member of John's group which were soon to evolve into the Beatles.

Following Stuart's death the Walker Art Gallery staged a posthumous exhibition of his works in May 1964, attended by 11,000 people.

There was an 'Art of the Beatles' exhibition at the Walker Art Gallery from 4th May to 30 September, 1984, attended by 50,000 people and in August 2002 an exhibition of Paul McCartney's paintings.

The Gallery possesses the Stuart painting 'Hamburg Painting No. 2', which Stuart painted in 1961.

Gambier Terrace, where John Lennon joined his mates Rod Murray and Stuart Sutcliffe

Ged Fleming

3 GAMBIER TERRACE, HILARY MANSIONS

Gambier Terrace is a row of houses overlooking St James' Mount and Gardens and the Liverpool Anglican Cathedral. The terrace was originally named after James Gambier, was designed by John Foster and is now part of the Rodney Street conservation area.

This Georgian Terrace once housed the Liverpool School of Art which I attended, along with Cynthia Powell (later Lennon), Les Chadwick (who took photos for me for Mersey Beat under the Pete Kaye name) and Fred O'Brien designer of several Beatles' plaques).

It was also to house a flat at Number 3 where John Lennon joined his mates Rod Murray and Stuart Sutcliffe. Other occupants included Rod Jones, Margaret 'Duckie' Duxbury and Margaret 'Diz' Morris.

Rod tells me: "I was going out with Duckie late 1958 to late 1959; I was still with her when we (Stu, Diz, Duckie and myself) went to Stratford to see Othello in June 1959. Diz and Duckie moved into Gambier from the start with Stu and myself, followed soon after by John in an 'I am only staying the odd night' way so he wouldn't have to pay up! But later he put it on a cash basis and was allocated a shelf in the kitchen. Duckie did not stay very long and as Diz and I had then got together she moved into the front room with me, Rod Jones took over the small front room that Diz and Duckie had shared. The flat was this time in my name and the rent was £3 per week paid monthly."

In his book 'Haunted Liverpool 5' author Tom Slemen writes of 'The Ghost of Gambier Terrace', suggesting that a ghost which people believe to be that of Stuart Sutcliffe, has been reported several times since 1965 at Number 3 Gambier Terrace. He quotes a man working for a postal delivery service who, in 1991 reported an apparition when he called at Gambier Terrace, stating that as he walked away he heard footsteps behind him, turned and saw a youth about 20-years-old, wearing sunglasses, narrow trousers, a polo neck sweater under a jacket and sporting sideburns. The youth suddenly disappeared before his eyes.

Frankly this report is too tenuous to be credible.

As is the story that Stuart slept in a coffin. Rod Murray says, "The coffin business is daft and I have tried to put it right on numerous occasions; it comes from the fact that Rod Jones in his flat in Percy Street had his bed in an alcove that was painted black and had plastic lily of the valley flowers and curtains on each side, very funereal!"

I was a frequent visitor to Gambier Terrace and was also witness to John and Stuart attempting to think of a new name for the group one evening.

They'd long since jettisoned the name the Quarry Men and at one time had called themselves the Moondogs, then Johnny & the Moondogs, Casey Jones had even suggested they call themselves Long John and the Silver Men. When we booked them for our art college dances I just referred to them as the college band.

It was Stuart who said they should think up a name similar to Buddy Holly's backing band the Crickets. Under the name the Quarry Men and at the college dances they had included a number of Holly's songs in their repertoire. An obvious next step was to think of the name of insects and they came up with beetles (Ironically enough, Holly had originally considered using the name Beetles for his band before deciding on the Crickets). I had believed at the time that it was the wordsmith John Lennon who came up with the 'a'.

On another occasion, on the weekend beginning Friday 24 June, 1960, after John, Stuart, Rod and I had visited Liverpool University to see Beat poet Royston Ellis, Stuart met him at the Jacaranda club and invited him to the Gambier Terrace flat where he was invited to stay for a few days.

They then trooped down to the Jacaranda and backed his poems in a Poetry-to-Rock session. Royston told me, "Unfortunately I don't remember what I performed at the Jacaranda and can only assume that we rehearsed at the flat beforehand. I based a chapter on the Jacaranda in a 1963 novel I wrote about a pop star called 'Myself For Fame' in which the Beatles feature as the Rythmettes.

"However, Paul told me in Paris when we met by chance in 2006 that he remembers one of the poems had the line 'Break me in easy' – he even recited it to me – so the poems came from my book 'Rave' published later in 1961. Incidentally, I dedicated my 1963 pamphlet of poems 'A Seaman's Suitcase' to 'Tony and Jet, Christine Keeler and the Beatles in admiration of their achievements.'"

While Royston was at the Gambier Terrace flat he introduced John, Stuart, Rod and I to our very first experience of a drug. He cracked open a Vick inhaler and showed us the strip of Benzedrine inside. It was nicknamed a 'spitball' and you chewed it. The amphetamine kept you awake all night in a state of excitement.

He told me, "Yes, the Vick inhaler story has become part of drug legend. I was shown how to do that by a singer who later became Neil Christian and his guitarist, who used to accompany me in those days, Jimmy Page."

By this time the group had adopted the name the Silver Beetles and when they showed the spelling to Royston he told me that he suggested then that they put an 'a' into the word, making it 'Beatles', inspired by the Beat

Generation in America. This wasn't anything to do with the term 'Beat Group' which hadn't yet become a notable terminology

Oddly enough, although they were billed as the Silver Beetles when they undertook a series of six consecutive Thursday night bookings at the Neston Institute, beginning 2 June 1960, a review of their appearance published in the Heswall and Neston News and Advertiser stated: "A Liverpool rhythm group, The Beatles, made their debut at Neston Institute on Thursday night." This was actually the very first time the name the Beatles was used in print, although the group didn't actually decide to settle on the name the Beatles until the following month.

Ellis recalled that in conversations with Paul he told him of his ambitions to be a 'paperback writer' and said that he used the phrase so often in his conversations, that perhaps Paul subconsciously recalled it when he came to write the song. The Record Mirror reported that Ellis was thinking of bringing a Liverpool group called the Beetles to London to back him on his poetry readings, but nothing came of it.

Royston tells me, "I recall discussing with John at the Gambier Terrace flat my plan to take John, Stuart, George and Paul to London to back me on my poetry reading performances. This was reported in the Record Mirror of 9 July 1960 – the first ever national musical press reference to 'the Beetles' with a follow-up in the next issue, 14 July 1960, in which I described the Beetles thus: "For some time I have been searching for a group to use regularly and I feel that the Beetles (most of them are Liverpool art students) fit the bill.

"Of course, they never got to London to back me but I do remember meeting Allan Williams in London and he said that John wanted me to go to Hamburg with them as compere. I declined and am alive to tell the tale!

"I asked John what name he was calling the group. He said the Beetles. I asked him how it was spelt and he said B-E-E-T-L-E-S. That's when I suggested that since they liked the beats and I was a beat poet, why not spell it with an A."

He also told me, "I recall cooking a meal at the flat one day which included frozen chicken pie. Somehow I managed to burn the chicken pie. It is that, I have always assumed, that gave rise to John's reference to 'a man on a flaming pie' suggesting they call themselves Beatles with an A – as you published in Mersey Beat the following year.

"John did make other references to me in subsequent writings, including 'Polythene Pam' and 'Paperback Writer' (based on my phrase "I want to be a paperback writer" which I stated when we were discussing what we wanted to be in life. I recall later, in Jersey, advising John how to get rid of crab lice, and he made a reference to this in one of his stories. A great and incredible man!"

Being witness to John and Stu thinking up their name early in 1960, it surprised me when some years ago, it began to be reported that the group had thought up the name after seeing the Marlon Brando film 'The Wild One' in which Lee Marvin briefly mentions a motorcycle gang called the Beetles.

No member of the Beatles saw this film, which was banned in Britain for 14 years. The 'Chronicle of the Cinema' in its entry on events of 1968, announced: "London. 15 February. Laslo Benedek's 'The Wild One' has at last been released here. It has been banned by the British Censors for 14 years due to the activities of a group of bikers in the film which were judged likely to incite violence among the young."

Why, I wondered, did this completely mythic story arise? Who was responsible for something which could so easily be disproved? It seemed that Beatles aide Derek Taylor was in America in the mid-Sixties and saw the film and asked George Harrison if they derived their name from the film, unaware that it had never been shown in Britain.

George, not being witness to John and Stuart originating the name, thought the story might be credible. In 'The Beatles Anthology' he is reported as saying "There was the Crickets who backed Buddy Holly, that similarity, but Stuart was really into Marlon Brando, and in the movie 'The Wild One' there is a scene where Lee Martin says, 'Johnny, we've been looking for you, the Beetles have missed you, all the Beetles have missed you.' Maybe John and Stuart were both thinking about it at the time."

They weren't. I was witness to the history. However, due to the 'Anthology' quote – and the book also included a photo of Marlon Brando, this seemed to give credence to the myth. Excuses to revive the myth were made, even when I was to point out on numerous occasions that when the Beatles decided on the name in 1960, they had never seen the movie.

Pauline Sutcliffe in her ghost-written book on Stuart called 'The Beatles Shadow' (a name which had actually been previously dubbed on Mal Evans); said Stuart had seen it at a film society. He hadn't. I ran the art college film society and booked the films.
"We weren't even aware of 'The Wild One' and Stuart was hooked on Zbigniew Cybulski because I'd booked Andrzej Wajda's film 'Ashes And Diamonds,' which impressed Stuart so much that he began to wear dark glasses like the anti-hero in the film. He was also more into James Dean than Marlon Brando.

So there we go, another myth bites the dust!

Other occupants of Gambier Terrace included Margaret 'Duckie' Duxbury

Ed Chapman

"I ASKED JOHN WHAT NAME HE WAS CALLING THE GROUP. HE SAID THE BEETLES …THAT'S WHEN I SUGGESTED THAT SINCE THEY LIKED THE BEATS AND I WAS A BEAT POET, WHY NOT SPELL IT WITH AN A."

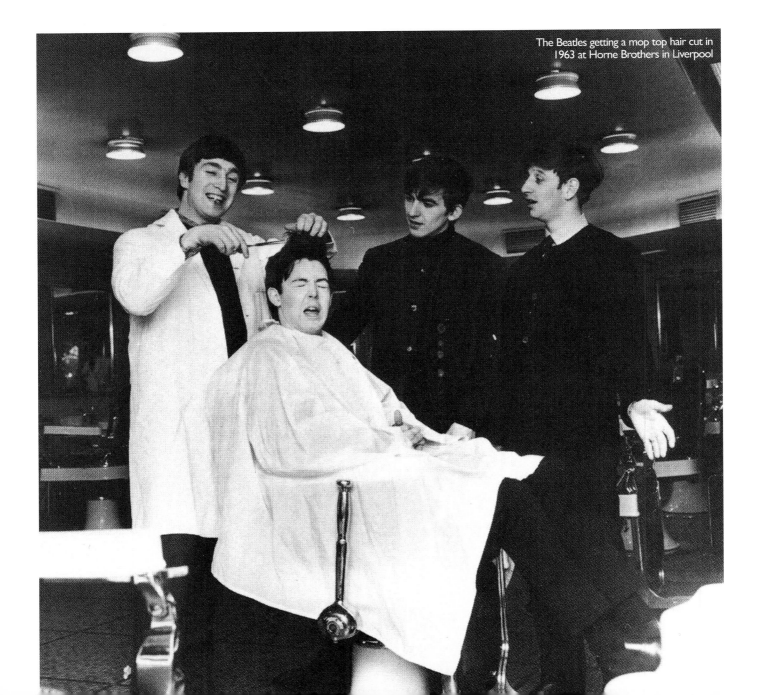

The Beatles getting a mop top hair cut in 1963 at Horne Brothers in Liverpool

A few months later came an incident which eventually led to Rod being evicted while John and Stu were in Germany. A journalist Peter Forbes and a photographer Harold Chapman began chatting to us in Ye Cracke.

They gave us different stories about the assignment they were on, resulting in me taking them to my house in Parliament Street to show them that it was nearly falling into the street. (It actually did this some time later – the wall of my bedroom collapsed and fell into the street and when I returned from college the entire street was cordoned off!)

But this wasn't of interest to them because it wasn't the series they were working on. They then told us one story about the difficulties of living on a student's grant and another about students influenced by the Beat Generation.

They were obviously put on to us by Allan Williams as members of the press were regulars at his club and he cultivated them in order to get publicity.

When they insisted on visiting the Gambier Terrace flat, Allan came along with them. Rod Murray, Rod Jones and Pete 'the Beat' McGrath were among those gathered in Rod's room.

I recall Williams and the newspaper men seemed dissatisfied that the room wasn't in a mess and suggested that it be roughed up; crumpling newspapers and laying beer bottles on the floor and such, making it look dishevelled.

As author Alan Clayson recounts in his book 'John Lennon': "The reporters from gutter tabloid 'The Sunday People' were shocked that the flat was clean, one of the residents had a job and wore a suit, and another resident said she'd be happy to invite her parents over for a meal. Not the story they were looking for! So Lennon and friends obliged them by making the place look a mess."

Neither John, Stu nor myself were in the photos that were taken. Rod tells me, "There were quite a lot of people there; I always thought that John and Stu were there. They are not in the well-known photo but that does not mean they were not there. Diz was not in the photo but was in the front room. The guy on the floor who looks like John is either Rod Jones or Pete the Beat. We moved my home-built lo-fi record player in to the studio for the photos."

Rod also told me: "The flat was well kept and clean, mainly by Diz and Duckie. We even had hot water in the bathroom! We painted the large front room which was used by all of us as a living room. The only untidy room was the studio that Stu and John shared."

Everyone should have realised something was going on by the request to dirty the place up as the photographer clicked away. As it turned out, Forbes and Chapman were doing a series on British Beatniks for the People newspaper, with a brief to sensationalise the series.

This resulted in a fit-up. On Sunday 24 July 1960, The People ran an exaggerated, incredibly inaccurate feature with a cover story, which then spread over two further pages, under the title 'This Is The Beatnik Horror.'

In part, the lurid account by Forbes read:

"Beatniks, according to the American 'teachers' are rebels against conventional society. They do not give a damn for anyone or anything – except themselves.

"How that works out in practice can be seen from the group that inhabits a three-roomed flat in decaying Gambier Terrace in the heart of Liverpool. There live Rod Jones, Rod Murray and a fluctuating number of their beatnik friends. Jones, 22, is at the local art college. Murray, who is a year older, has just left.

"The squalor that surrounds these well-educated youngsters in unbelievable. When I visit their 'home' the only furniture I saw in their living room was a decaying armchair and a table which could not have been seen for debris. Boxes, newspapers, milk bottles, bits of orange peel, beer and spirits bottles, tubes of paint, cups, plastic beacons from zebra crossings. Clothes, lumps of cement and plaster of Paris – these were just a few of the things that lay ankle deep across the floor."

There was a quote from Rod Murray in which he was alleged to have said, "At our last place, we burned all the furniture because we didn't have any money to buy coal. We were very lucky. We found a whole cellar full of furniture belonging to our landlady. So we started burning our way through that."

Rod Jones is purported to have said, "We don't believe in work – it's just for mugs. My only interests are girls and poetry." However, when Rod saw the muck-raking feature in the People he abandoned the flat.

Rod Murray was to comment, "An awful lot of stuff in that article was either blatant untruths or so distorted."
Ever since, people have reported Number 3 Gambier Terrace at the time as being a place of squalor and there were even reports that Stuart slept in a coffin!

Living underneath, in the basement of Gambier Terrace were artist Sam Walsh and writer Johnny Byrne, both originally from Ireland together with

"THE BEATLES DID PRACTICE IN THE STUDIO AND THE 'NOISE' THEY MADE WAS PART OF THE REASON WE WERE SLUNG OUT."

a genuine beatnik called Spike Hawkins. When Rod was about to be evicted and bailiffs dumped a lot of John and Stu's work to the rear of the premises, Johnny took it and burnt it on the fire.

He was to recall: "Outside were all these paintings of Lennon's – the landlord came and the Beatles hadn't paid their rent and the paintings were thrown out into the backyard where they were rotting. And I went out and got all these paintings and I burnt I don't know how many to keep us warm."

Johnny must have burnt John's work with glee because he didn't like him and was to say, "I hated Lennon. Oh yes. Lennon's no hero of mine. I cannot separate people and what they do from what they are. Lennon was unmitigatedly evil as far as I was concerned. Perhaps evil is too strong a word, and I want to believe that people can change, but he treated his wife Cynthia and his kid abysmally."

Johnny was later to become a prominent British television scriptwriter launching series such as 'All Creatures Great And Small' and 'Heartbeat.' Sam had many acclaimed paintings to his credit, including one of Paul McCartney which he captioned 'Mike's Brother.' Sadly, Sam died in 1989 and Johnny in 2008.

Of course, it wasn't the Beatles' flat as some writers intimate. Once Rod and Stu had moved in, John wanted to leave Menlove Avenue and join them, telling his aunt "I feel like a baby living at home."

She gave him his grant money and allowed him to leave. The money ran out after four weeks and he returned to Menlove, desperate for a decent meal. After a short stay, when Mimi gave him some more money, he returned to Gambier Terrace.

Rod was to recall, "John never had any money when rent day came around, so you took whatever was offered." He was referring to the various odds and sods which John gave him in lieu of the rent such as a cigarette lighter and a pewter tankard.

The Sunday People article and the noise the group had made from rehearsals were the final step and Rod was evicted. Stu and John were in Germany at the time and Rod Jones had left soon after the People article was published.

Rod Murray had received a letter from the estate agents which began: "We've received a number of complaints regarding the late night parties and excessive noise coming from your flat. We regret that if further complaints are made we shall have no alternative but to terminate your tenancy and take possession of the flat."
Rod mentions, "The Beatles did practice in the studio and the 'NOISE' they made was part of the reason we were slung out."

In fact, with virtually everyone gone, Rod could no longer afford to pay the rent anyway. He informed Millie Sutcliffe who came along, paid Rod money towards Stuart's share of the rent and took Stu's belongings, along with a number of items of John's, which included a chest of drawers with John's clothing which Millie's husband Charles threw out when he discovered they belonged to John.

John Lennon and Paul McCartney
on stage at the Casbah in 1959

CHAPTER 5
THE BIRTH OF THE BEATLES

THE CASBAH

Which Liverpool club with six letters, beginning with 'C' could be known as 'the birthplace of the Beatles,'?

The immediate answer would generally be 'Cavern', yet the 'Casbah' has a strong case for claiming that title. If it hadn't been for the Casbah, there probably wouldn't have been a group that became the Beatles.

The Casbah is situated at 8 Hayman's Green, West Derby. Former Beatles drummer Pete Best was to tell me, "We have always said that the Casbah was the birthplace of the Beatles. I know that the Cavern in Mathew Street has now announced that it's 'the birthplace of the Beatles' but as far as I'm concerned, it was the Casbah. If it wasn't for the club the Beatles might never have got together again and what happened later wouldn't have transpired."

The Quarry Men, John's original skiffle group, had ceased performing in January 1959. As the months passed and there was no sign of the group being revived, George Harrison joined another group, the Les Stewart Quartet, who had a residency at Lowlands, a club in Hayman's Green, West Derby.

Also situated in Hayman's Green, at Number 8, was a 15-room Victorian house, which the Best family had moved into after the Second World War. They comprised John and Mona Best and their sons Peter and Rory.

As there were so many friends calling in to see her sons and as they wanted a meeting place of their own, Mo Best suggested that they could redecorate the cellars and turn them into a club. There was plenty of room as the basement comprised seven adjoining rooms.

"EACH SATURDAY THE QUARRY MEN APPEARED ON STAGE AT 8.00PM."

The idea developed and she began to have in mind something like the nearby Lowlands club, with live groups at the weekend, with the club also open during the week as a coffee bar where the youngsters could dance to a jukebox.

The idea for the Casbah came after watching the television programme 'The Friday Night Special' and seeing the 2 I's coffee bar in London.

Work began on the decoration, with Mo, Peter, Rory and a number of friends, including a girl called Ruth Morrison. When Mo said they'd have to find a group, Ruth suggested the Les Stewart Quartet, who played at Lowlands club.

Ruth was one of George Harrison's earliest girlfriends. Ken Brown was to say: "George had never really been too keen on girls. He was only 16 and at the Liverpool Institute with Paul McCartney. Later, he seemed to go head over heels for Ruth."

The couple were only in the bloom of first love, holding hands and kissing, but nothing further than that.

Ken was also to recall: "It was the summer of 1958 and George and I were playing in the Les Stewart Quartet with a chap called Skinner. We spent hours practicing in the Lowlands Club, Hayman's Green. We would have probably gone on playing at clubs, but for George's girlfriend, Ruth. One evening the three of us were sitting in the Lowlands, drinking coffee, moaning about the fact that we had nowhere regular to play when Ruth suggested we see Mrs Best at the Casbah. She promised that the Les Stewart Quartet would play at the club when it opened."

George and Ken met with Mrs Best, although it was Ken who seemed most enthusiastic about the project and it was Ken who began to spend his spare time helping to convert the cellars into a club and spent weekends working there with the result that group leader Stewart argued with him about the amount of time he spent helping out there and he refused to take on the residency.

Ken and George then had to make a decision, with Ken later to recall, "As we were walking down the road, I turned to George and said: 'We can't let Mrs Best down now. Let's try and get a group together ourselves. Do you know anyone?'

George told him about two friends he used to play with and set out to tell John and Paul that there was an offer of a residency if they joined him and Ken. But for that sequence of events, the Quarry Men might never have re-formed, which meant there would never have been a group who were to become the Beatles.

In the cellars, bench seats and a counter were fitted in and Mrs Best painted a dragon on the ceiling. There was a table in the foyer where Mo would issue the tickets and there were tables and a fireplace, espresso coffee machines and in a small room a bar which sold coffee, sweets, soft drinks, hot dogs and crisps.

George turned up with John Lennon and his girlfriend Cynthia Powell and they helped with painting the walls shortly before the official opening. John used gloss paint on the walls instead of putting on an undercoat and the paint was not completely dry on opening night.

The conversion and transformation of the basement rooms into a cellar club took two months. Mona's favourite film at the time was 'Algiers', which starred Charles Boyer. People attempted to mimic him by saying 'Come with me to the Casbah' whenever the film was mentioned, although that line of dialogue was never in the movie. Mona settled on calling the club the Casbah.

When the club was officially opened on Saturday 29 August 1959, the resident band was the Quarry Men. The doors opened at 7.30 and each Saturday the Quarry Men appeared on stage at 8.00pm. Membership was two shillings and sixpence (12 1/2d) and entrance at the door cost one shilling (5p). During the first year the club enrolled 1,000 members.

Mo had also invited the local newspaper – the West Derby Reporter – to the club and they ran a story headed, 'Kasbah (sic) Has A New Meaning For Local Teenagers.'

Roag Best

"IF IT HADN'T BEEN FOR THE CASBAH, THERE PROBABLY WOULDN'T HAVE BEEN A GROUP THAT BECAME THE BEATLES."

Pete and Mona Best at the Casbah

Part of the story, under the heading 'Guitar Group' read: "Three of the boys, Kenneth Brown of 149 Storrington Avenue, Norris Green, David Hughes, 119 Blackmoor Drive, West Derby and Douglas Jenkins, 28 Cottesbrook Road, Norris Green, went to the cellars from their jobs each evening and helped with the conversion at weekends.

"Kenneth Brown is also a member of a guitar group which entertains the club members on Saturday nights. The other members of the group, who call themselves the Quarry Men, travel from the south end of the city to play.

"They are: John Lennon, Menlove Avenue, Woolton, Paul McCartney, Forthlin Road, Allerton and George Harrison, Upton Green, Speke. During the week members take their own records or play those provided by Mrs Best. There is even a room for the energetic who wish to dance."

Cynthia was in the audience and is featured in the photograph taken at the time by the local newspaper. Dorothy Rhone, the pretty little blonde with the elfin looks was also present at the Casbah and became Paul McCartney's first real steady girlfriend.

The four-man line-up of John Lennon, Paul McCartney, George Harrison and Ken Brown played without a drummer, using Brown's ten-watt amplifier, and they received £3 a night between them. Among the numbers played were 'Three Cool Cats' sung by John and 'Long Tall Sally' sung by Paul. Brown played a Hofner guitar.

This line-up played the club each Saturday on 29 August, 5, 12, 19 and 26 September, 3 and 10 October. On 10 October Brown arrived at the club, but he had a bad cold. Mrs Best told him he could help out and paid him a quarter of the group's fee, even though he didn't play.

John, Paul and George were furious and stalked out of the club, abandoning their residency. Brown encouraged Pete Best to form a group with him, ironically calling it the Blackjacks, which was the Quarry Men's original name.

Mo bought Pete a drum kit from Rushworth & Dreaper. They recruited Bill Barlow on bass and Chas Newby on lead and, as the Blackjacks, took over the residency and the club went from strength to strength, building up a loyal membership and booking

groups such as Rory Storm & the Hurricanes and Derry & the Seniors.

John, Paul and George didn't return to the Casbah until 3 August 1960 when they dropped into the club after their booking at the Grosvenor Ballroom, Wallasey, had been cancelled.

They had already been booked for their Hamburg debut, although they still hadn't found a drummer. They noticed Pete playing with the Blackjacks and admired the blue mother-of-pearl drum kit and Paul McCartney phoned him to invite him to audition with them. He did – and was invited to join the group.

The first gig they did on their return from Hamburg was the Casbah Club on 17 December when Pete arranged for them to have a temporary bass player, Chas Newby, as Stuart Sutcliffe was still in Germany.

Pete and Mona Best now took charge of all the Beatles' bookings and, in addition to the Casbah gigs, formed Casbah Promotions to run dances at St John's Hall, Tuebrook and Knotty Ash Village Hall, where they booked the Beatles regularly.

Their 1961 Casbah appearances took place on 8, 15, 22 and 29 January; 12, 19 and 26 February; 5 and 19 March; 6, 13 and 27 August; 10 and 24 September; 22 October; 19 and 24 November; 3 and 17 December. Dates in 1962 were on 7, 14, 21 and 28 January; 4, 11, 18 and 25 February; 4, 11, 18 and 25 March; 1 and 7 April; 24 June. The latter saw the Beatles final appearance at the club which was closed down a few days later following a death in the Best family.

The Beatles gathered together on the Casbah premises on 10 December 1961 with Brian Epstein and signed their first contract with him. Brian then realised they hadn't signed over a postage stamp, so it wasn't legally binding. The second contract was signed at NEMS.

The Casbah club played an important part in the formative career of the Beatles. If it had not opened, the Quarry Men would probably not have re-formed and there would have been no Beatles.

The club provided them with their first residency and a base with regular money when times were tight. It also provided them with their first regular drummer, Pete Best, their first road manager, Frank Garner – and their regular road manager Neil Aspinall: which gives it solid provenance to be dubbed 'the birthplace of the Beatles.'

Ken Brown, who suffered from emphysema, died in June 2010; sadly Mona Best died in hospital on 9 September 1988 following a heart attack after a long illness; after her romance with George ended, Ruth Morrison decided on the career path of a nurse and moved to Birmingham to pursue it.

The Casbah itself was listed as a Grade II Heritage building and was re-opened as a tourist attraction in 2008. What is most remarkable is that it remains exactly as it was when the Quarrymen originally had their residency there.

Paul McCartney was to say, "I think it's a good idea to let people know about The Casbah. They know about the Cavern, they know about some of those things, but the Casbah was the place where it all started. We helped paint it and stuff. We looked upon it as our personal club."

The English Heritage representative was to comment: "The basement Casbah Club rooms are historically significant because they represent tangible evidence of the Beatles' formation, their growth in popularity and their enduring cultural influence throughout the world.

"The club survives in a remarkably well-preserved condition since its closure in 1962, with wall and ceiling paintings of spiders, dragons, rainbows and stars by original band members along with 1960's musical equipment, amplifiers and original chairs. We know of no other survival like it in Liverpool or indeed anywhere else."

The other Hayman's Green venue Lowlands was built in 1846 and over the years has had many uses, ranging from a family home to a temporary base for the Inland Revenue. In the late 1950s and up to 1966, Lowlands housed the Pillar Club, where many local groups performed including the Quarry Men, Gerry & the Pacemakers, the Searchers, Hollies and Billy Kramer & the Coasters.

The building was recently refurnished at a cost of £1.2million.

Ged Fleming

Plaque commemorating the birthplace of the Beatles at the Casbah coffee club, established August 29, 1959

"THE CASBAH WAS THE PLACE WHERE IT ALL STARTED . . .WE LOOKED UPON IT AS OUR PERSONAL CLUB." *PAUL MCCARTNEY*

THE CAVERN

Disc jockey Bob Wooler was to dub the Cavern 'The Best of Cellars.' The Mathew Street club was where the Beatles appeared almost 280 times over a two and a half year period and they performed there for the last time on 3 August 1963 for a fee of £300.

That evening, Beatles manager Brian Epstein told Wooler that one day the Beatles would be back – but they had played their last Cavern performance. Originally the premises comprised a group of cellars below seven-storey warehouses, which, during the last war, had been used as air-raid shelters. For a while wines and spirits were stored there and in 1958, Alan Sytner, son of a local doctor, noticed that the premises were empty.

Sytner had been running jazz nights at a nearby restaurant. He'd recently been to Paris and was impressed by a jazz cellar he'd visited called La Caveau Francais Jazz club. He took over the lease of the basement and the club officially opened as the Cavern on 16 January 1957 with local jazz band the Merseysippi topping the bill.

There were three long arches with a stage at the end of the central aisle, where rows of wooden seats were placed. Patrons danced in the outer aisles. Only soft drinks were served and initially just traditional jazz was presented at weekends. Then skiffle was presented each Wednesday and modern jazz each Thursday.

Rock 'n' roll was banned.

The Quarry Men's first Cavern gig was set in motion by John's close friend Nigel Walley, who John often referred to as 'Whalloggs'.

Nigel lived in Vale Road, to the rear of where John lived in Menlove Avenue and in the same road as another friend, Ivan Vaughan. When John formed his group the Quarry Men, Nigel was invited to play tea chest bass, although he says he only played it occasionally, with Ivan being the main bass player.

The group needed someone to get the gigs sorted out and promote the group. No one really wanted to do it, but John asked Nigel who then set about getting them work. He placed a card in

"THE RECORD FOR BEATLE
WAITING WENT TO TWO
YOUNGSTERS IN 1963 WHO
QUEUED OUTSIDE THE CLUB
FOR ONE MONTH TO ENSURE
A FRONT ROW SEAT."

The Beatles on stage at the Cavern

the window of a Woolton sweet shop at 2d per week, took small ads in the Liverpool Echo and the Daily Post and even had professional 'Quarry Men' cards printed:

COUNTRY. WESTERN. ROCK 'N' ROLL. SKIFFLE
THE QUARRY MEN
OPEN FOR ENGAGEMENTS

When the Quarry Men were deciding on their repertoire, Nigel says, "They picked out records by Buddy Holly, Bill Haley and popular rock and roll numbers of the time. Elvis Presley's 'Heartbreak Hotel' was a number John was particularly struck on. We saw Buddy Holly live with the Crickets when he appeared on the Liverpool Empire. It was one of the highlights of my life.

"We picked the tunes from records that were readily available in the shops. That story about Liverpool groups getting their repertoires from records brought in by merchant seamen is a myth, although lots of Liverpool men went to sea. Pete Shotton's brother Ernie was in the Navy."

When Nigel used to go round to John's house and ask his Aunt Mimi "Where's John?" "Where do you think, in his bedroom playing his guitar", she'd say. Nigel would go up and sit on the bed while John would be playing. "He'd write a song in a few minutes" said Nigel. "I didn't think much of it at the time.

At the time Nigel was apprentice golf professional at Lee Park Golf Club. "Lee Park Gold Club was a Jewish golf club," he says. "If you weren't Jewish you couldn't get in."

One of the members was Dr Sytner, whose son Alan ran the Cavern Club, which was then a jazz venue that occasionally booked local skiffle groups as supports. Nigel asked Dr Sytner if he could persuade Alan to book the Quarry Men on the Cavern. He was told that they'd have to see the group before they could be booked on the Cavern and he suggested that the group perform at the golf club first. If they were any good, then Alan would book them on his club.

They were told that as the appearance would be something of an audition, they wouldn't be paid. However, they would have all the drink that they wanted, a slap-up meal and the hat would be passed around. When they completed their performance they did

have lots of drink, a slap-up meal – and the hat, when passed around, brought them more money than they'd ever received from a gig before. Not only that, Alan Sytner liked the group and booked them in the Cavern. They appeared there on 7 August 1957, although John was to upset Sytner when they did appear, by singing the Elvis Presley numbers 'Hound Dog' and 'Blue Suede Shoes' at a time when rock 'n' roll was banned at the Cavern. A furious Sytner sent a note on stage: "Cut out the bloody rock!"

Although Nigel acted as manager, when he didn't actually perform with them on tea chest bass, Paul McCartney got understandably upset and said that he should take a reduced fee. When the Quarry Men made their debut at the Cavern, Paul wasn't present as he was away at a scout camp.

By 1959 Sytner had got married and moved to London, leaving the running of the club to his father.

Financially, the Cavern wasn't faring well and Sytner decided to sell it. He found a buyer close to home – Ray McFall, the Sytner family accountant, who purchased the club on 1 October 1959 for £2,750. Ray continued the rock 'n' roll ban.

When Rory Storm & the Hurricanes, with drummer Ringo Starr, were booked as a skiffle group, they dared to play 'Whole Lotta Shakin'. Not only did McFall fine them, but the jazz audience pelted them with coins. After the performance the group picked the coins from the stage and found it added to more than their fine and fee put together.

By 1960 the jazz audience had waned and McFall decided on a radical departure – the introduction of rock 'n' roll at lunchtime sessions. This proved popular and on Wednesday 25 May 1960 the first rock 'n' roll evening was presented with two top local Liverpool bands Cass & the Cassanovas and Rory Storm & the Hurricanes.

The Beatles made their debut at a lunchtime session on 21 February 1961 and their evening debut on 21 March 1961. The first Cavern evening, which had no jazz at all, took place on Sunday 1 July 1961 featuring the Beatles, the Swinging Bluejeans, Gene Vincent and Sounds Incorporated.

When the Swinging Bluejeans arrived for an evening session they

were delighted to see the biggest Cavern queue they'd ever witnessed. Inside the club there were only a handful of people. When they asked if the crowd was going to be allowed in, they were told the queue was for the Beatles the following night.

The record for Beatle waiting went to two youngsters in 1963 – Pamela Black and Carol Lloyd. When the Beatles were due to appear at the Cavern, Pam and Carol queued outside the club for ONE MONTH to ensure a front row seat.

The girls left their spot at 10pm and resumed their place early the next morning. There was no fear of queue jumping because there was an unwritten law among the Beatles fans that the early queuers secured the best seats.

Even when the Beatles no longer appeared there, the Cavern success story continued. There was a group called the Caverners, a dance called the Cavern Stomp and a regular weekly radio show called Sunday Night at the Cavern. There was a Junior Cavern Club each Saturday afternoon for 13 – 16 year olds with the prominent sign: "Adults not admitted unless accompanied by children!"
TV cameramen from America, France, Sweden and German focused their cameras on the heady atmosphere, radio teams came from India, Russian and Canada and celebrities who dropped into the club included film stars such as Anna Neagle, musicians such as Chet Atkins, classical conductor Arthur Feidler and dozens of others.

A management/agency Cavern Artists Ltd was formed and when McFall bought the premises next door and extended the club, he also opened a Cavern Sound recording studio.

During the alterations he sold the original stage as 'Beatleboard', with the proceeds going to Oxfam.

Unfortunately, too many enterprises overextended his capital. Local Cavernites wanted to keep the club open, but the bailiffs were called in. The irate fans staged a sit-in. Frieda Kelly, the Beatles fan club secretary, took part in the siege by blockading the stairway of the Cavern with chairs. Eventually the police moved in and removed the struggling inhabitants.

Joe Davey who ran a local café that had been frequented by the

Beatles acquired the club. Prime Minister Harold Wilson officially reopened it on 23 January 1966, while Ken Dodd and local MP Bessie Braddock were present. The Beatles were unable to attend, but sent a telegram.

The Cavern changed hands again and was taken over by another local club-owner, Roy Adams. Although he ran the club successfully, Roy couldn't fight the local bureaucracy. The corporation decided they needed to fit an extraction duct for the underground railway in the premises and Adams was given notice to quit. The club was forced to close on 27 March 1973 and bulldozers razed the site. The Cavern itself was buried in rubble and when the railway work had been completed, the site was turned into a car park.

Following John Lennon's death, Liverpool architect David Backhouse approached Royal Life Insurance to develop the site. £9 million was spent on the scheme. Backhouse designed the basic plans for the complex in two days, producing an original design of a structure seven storeys high. He also included provision for the restructuring of a new Cavern club.

The original bricks of the club were still buried below the car park in the packed earth and a number of the original bricks were used in the construction.

For some reason the new Cavern was built parallel to Mathew Street, in contrast to the original, which had been built at a right angle to the street. As a result, instead of merely walking down eighteen steps into a club, a new entrance with a large spiral staircase had to be constructed.

Cynthia Lennon was asked to provide a design for the terracotta tiles that would face parts of the new building. On 25 April, 1984 she unveiled a small commemorative plaque, placed on an outside wall, inscribed 'To John' and containing the lyrics to 'In My Life'.

The Cavern still holds enormous power for old and young music fans alike.

Indeed, every year on August Bank holiday weekend, over half a million people flock to Liverpool to witness 130 international bands perform at the Mathew Street Festival and on the original Cavern site – and to remember the place that changed their lives forever.

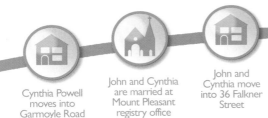

Cynthia Powell
moves into
Garmoyle Road

John and Cynthia
are married at
Mount Pleasant
registry office

John and
Cynthia move
into 36 Falkner
Street

CHAPTER 6
ALL YOU NEED IS LOVE

93 GARMOYLE ROAD, L15

Cynthia had been staying in Menlove Avenue with John's Aunt Mimi, but the two just couldn't get on together and Cynthia decamped to stay with her aunt Tess. As it was such a distance from the art college and because there wasn't really enough room there, Cynthia decided to look for a flat on her own and settled at this address, just off Smithdown Road, in 1962, also ostensibly so that she and John, who was currently in Hamburg, could enjoy more undisturbed intimate relations.

Cynthia was to describe the flat in her second biography: "For fifty shillings a week I had a grubby room, with a one-bar electric fire to heat it, a minute one-ring cooker, a single-bed, an ancient chair and a moth-eaten rug. I had to put a shilling in the meter if I wanted hot water for a bath in the shared bathroom and even then the water was barely ankle deep."

On Cynthia's invitation, Paul's girlfriend Dot Rhone was initially going to share the room with Cynthia, but John objected, so she rented the adjoining room. As this room was the largest one, Cynthia moved into that and Dot took over the room Cynthia had been staying in.

This was the address at which Cynthia and John conceived Julian and where Paul ended his relationship with Dot.

One evening Dot had just washed her hair and had put it in rollers. She was dressed in an old sweater and a pair of her mother's bloomers when Paul arrived. He took her into her room and told her that their affair was over. Dot was heart-broken. She packed her bags and went back to her parents' home.

Within a year of the break-up, Dot emigrated to Canada and the following year she married a German businessman, Werner Becker.

The house in Garmoyle Road where
Cynthia lived with Paul McCartney's
girlfriend Dot Rhone

John joins Cynthia Lennon at
Heathrow Airport after the
Beatles' Australasia tour

64 MOUNT PLEASANT

This former Georgian Town House was once the Mount Pleasant
Registry Office where John and Cynthia were married on
Thursday 23 August. 1963.

It wasn't the same registry office where John's parents were
married, as a lot of people suppose. Alfred Lennon and Julia
Stanley were wed on 3 December 1938 in the registry office at
Bolton Street.

The marriage between John and Cynthia took place because she
had informed him she was pregnant and in those days, when such
things occurred, getting married was generally 'the right thing to
do.' John told Brian Epstein of the turn of events and it was Brian
who arranged for a special licence for them and sent a chauffeur-
driven car to pick her up at her Garmoyle Street apartment.

On arrival in Mount Pleasant she found her brother Tony, with his
wife Marjorie, Brian, John, Paul and George. Ringo, who had joined
the group only several days earlier, was not invited. Cynthia was
dressed in a purple and black check two-piece suit, a white frilly
high-necked blouse, which had been a present from Astrid
Kirchherr, black shoes and a handbag while Brian, the best man,
wore a pin-striped suit and John, Paul and George all wore black
suits with white shirts and black ties.

The group was ushered into the room where the ceremony was
to take place and Cynthia observed how dour the Registrar
looked. She also noticed, through a window, that a workman was
in the yard of the next door building, holding a pneumatic drill.

The service itself was concluded in a matter of minutes, but from
the onset the workman started up the drill and the noise was
deafening.

The former registry office in Mount Pleasant where the Lennons were married

One funny incident occurred when the registrar asked the groom to step forward and George did so, although the registrar didn't appreciate the joke. Commenting on their wedding several years later, Cynthia wrote: "John had not only gained a headache, he had gained a wife and the promise of a child in only eight months – possibly a bigger headache."

Absent from the ceremony was John's Aunt Mimi, leading John to say, "I went in the day before to tell Mimi. I said Cyn was having a baby, we were getting married tomorrow, did she want to come? She just let out a groan." However, it was Mimi who gave John £10 for him to buy Cynthia the wedding ring.

He also commented, "There was a drill going on all the time outside the Register Office. I couldn't hear a word the bloke was saying. Then we went across the road and had a chicken dinner. "It was all a laugh."

Witnesses James Paul McCartney and Marjorie Joyce Powell signed the certificate and as the party emerged into Mount Pleasant the heavens burst and it poured with rain as they ran down the hill towards Reece's Restaurant at the corner of Parker Street and Leigh Street to their wedding breakfast, which was hosted by Brian Epstein, although Tony and Marjorie couldn't join them as they had attended the ceremony during their lunch break.

Arriving at the restaurant on the first floor they were too late to beat the lunchtime crowds of office workers as they ate a set lunch comprising soup, chicken and trifle.
The premises were unlicensed and the couple were toasted with water.

There were plans to demolish the Mount Pleasant building, but they were dropped due to local opposition. The building became the offices of the Merseyside Racial Equality Council.

36 FALKNER STREET

Brian Epstein's wedding gift to John and Cynthia was the use of a flat he had at this address in Liverpool 8, which, incidentally, was only a few doors away from the house where art college model June Furlong lived.

It was also near to the flat of Brian's drama coach Helen Lindsay. At the wedding lunch in Reece's he suggested that John and Cynthia couldn't live in the room at Garmoyle Street and offered them this flat, which he claimed he used to entertain clients. Brian still lived at home in Queens Drive but used the premises for his private liaisons and rented it during 1961 and 1962 for £16 a month.

The couple moved in that evening, with Brian helping Cynthia to collect her things from Garmoyle Street and John picking up what he needed from Menlove Avenue.

It was certainly an improvement for Cynthia from the previous premises as it was nicely furnished and had a kitchen, bathroom, sitting room and a small walled garden.

Cynthia was to recall, "The only snag was that our bedroom was situated at the front of the house overlooking Falkner Street. Access to the rest of the flat was only by going through the main hall and past the front door which was used by all the other tenants of the building – very inconvenient when in need of the bathroom during the night. Anyone could wander in through the front door and walk from the street into our rooms if the door was open. It all made me very nervous at times, especially when John was away on tour."

Beatles manager Brian Epstein, whose wedding gift to John and Cynthia was the use of his flat in Falkner Street

She was also to describe one particular incident which occurred at midnight. She'd retired to bed and John had just locked up when the front door bell began to ring. As no one answered it, John opened the front door and was confronted by two rough-looking characters who demanded to see someone named Carol. John told them no one of that name lived there. He closed the door and returned to the flat.

A few minutes later someone began battering the flat door violently. The roughs began to shout, "We know she's there, you dirty ponce. We'll bloody tear you apart when we get our hands on you. You bloody hand her over or else!"

Cynthia was so frightened she began screaming and shouted out that her name was Cynthia, there was no one named Carol in the flat and that she was three months pregnant. There was some mumbling from the other side of the door and the roughs left.

Cynthia was quite lonely there as John continued travelling with the group immediately after the wedding. However, it was while the couple were residing in Falkner Street that John wrote 'Do You Want to Know A Secret?'

John was to comment, "I was in the first apartment I'd ever had that wasn't shared by fourteen other students – gals and guys at art school. I'd just married Cyn, and Brian Epstein gave us his secret little apartment that he kept in Liverpool for his sexual liaisons separate from his home life. And he let Cyn and I have that apartment."

However, at this time the Beatles were becoming more in demand and John was away a great deal of the time. Cynthia became frightened when she woke up one morning to find herself losing blood, so she called her brother Tony who arranged for a doctor to examine her and he recommended bed rest. Cynthia took his advice seriously, remaining in bed for three days, never leaving the room, using a bucket for a toilet and a kettle to make herself some tea. The bleeding had stopped by the time John returned home.

John and Cynthia then went to see Mimi at Mendips and it was agreed that they would move back there. With John away so much and about to venture on another trip to Hamburg, it was felt that she shouldn't be alone in case of an emergency.

"I'D JUST MARRIED CYN, AND BRIAN EPSTEIN GAVE US HIS SECRET LITTLE APARTMENT THAT HE KEPT IN LIVERPOOL."

Jim Gretty from the famous Hessy musical instrument store

Bill Harry

FRANK HESSY'S STORE

On 27 August 1957 John accompanied his Aunt Mimi to Frank Hessy's musical instruments store at 62 Stanley Street, in Liverpool city centre. He'd talked her into buying him a new Hofner Club 40 guitar. Mimi arranged to purchase the instrument and Jim Gretty was the salesman who sold Mimi the guitar.

Mimi recalled, "I thought I would teach him a lesson by getting him one. I thought that the novelty would wear off soon, and he would forget about it. So one Saturday we went down to Hessy's shop in Liverpool, and I bought him one there. It cost me fourteen pounds. Fourteen pounds!

"That was a lot of money in those days. I begrudged paying it on a guitar for him, but I thought that if it keeps him quiet, then there's no harm done. He would even stand in front of his bedroom mirror with the guitar pretending to be that man Elvis Presley."

Mimi is also alleged to have said to John "The guitar's all very well, John, but you can't make a living out of it."

When John later had a Rickenbacker 325 he modified it while he was in Hessy's store by replacing the vibrato unit.

On 20 November 1959 George Harrison went into Hessy's shop hoping to purchase a Stratocaster guitar. Unfortunately, Hessy didn't have one, so George ended up with a three-pickup Futurama costing £55. The name had been given to it by Selmer, who had imported the guitars, originally called Grazioso Resonet from Czechoslovakia.

Stuart Sutcliffe obtained his Hofner President Bass guitar from Hessy's. He didn't buy it outright with the £65 he'd received for selling his painting to John Moores, as legend has it.

Instead, like most musicians who bought their instruments in Liverpool in those days, it was on hire purchase and while in

Left: Lennon's Rickenbacker guitar
while on show in Cavern Walks

Germany he wrote to his mother telling her not to forget to keep up the payments.

When Brian Epstein became manager of the Beatles he paid all the outstanding sums on the Beatles guitars to Hessy, which amounted to £200 – translated into thousands of pounds today.

The store owner Frank Hessleberg was from a Lithuanian Jewish family and had opened his original branch in Manchester Street.

After moving into Stanley Street, in addition to his main salesman Jim Gretty, Hessy's wife operated the cash register and attended the accessories counter. Frank's daughter, together with her husband Bernard Michaelson, also worked in the store during the Sixties.

The Stanley Street store finally closed down in 1995. The manager at the time was Colin Benn, sadly to die following a routine operation.

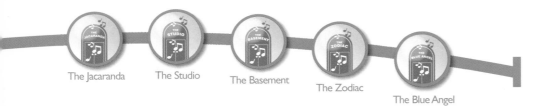

CHAPTER 7
MERSEY BEAT

THE JACARANDA

A coffee club at 23 Slater Street, Liverpool L1, which was opened by Allan Williams in September 1958.

At the time coffee bars were fashionable and this particular area of Liverpool was honeycombed with them.

Quite close to the Jacaranda was a coffee bar called the Studio, frequented by models and students from Liverpool College of Art; local painter Yankiel Feather ran the Basement, directly to the rear of Mount Pleasant Register Office where John and Cynthia were married (when told to leave because he was making disruptive noise on the piano, John took his keys and scored them across one of Yankiel's paintings on his way out).

Also in Mount Pleasant was Streates, where poetry readings were held with poets such as Roger McGough and Phil Tasker. 50 yards from the Jac, in Duke Street, were the Zodiac and Boomerang coffee bars – and there were many more.

Allan saw an advertisement in the Liverpool Echo which read "suitable premises for a club" and went to Slater Street. The premises to let were formerly occupied by Owens Watch Repair Shop and the lease was owned by a man in the sweetshop next door who demanded an extra £150 for 'goodwill and fittings.' Allan raised the money and managed to engage a group of West Indians to play in a steel band offering them ten shillings (50p) each.

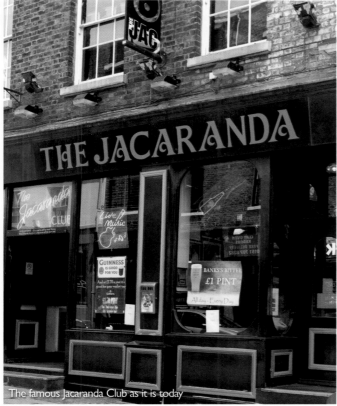

The famous Jacaranda Club as it is today

Shortly before opening the club, Allan had been trying to think up a suitable name. He eventually decided he'd call it the Samurai because he'd recently seen the film 'The Seven Samurai', when a friend, Bill Coward, who'd just read a book called 'The Jacaranda Tree', suggested Jacaranda.

The clientele was mixed – solicitors, doctors, art students, musicians – and two of the girls who served there as waitresses, Mary Larkin and Terry Sharrock, found themselves on the cover on the first issue of Mersey Beat after their photograph had been taken with rock 'n' roll star Gene Vincent. Soon after it opened, John, Stuart, Rod and I became regulars. We got to know many of the people who dropped in: Casey Jones, Adrian Barber, Rory

Storm, Johnny Guitar and people like Pete 'the Beat' McGrath.

In the attic room a young man sold second-hand records. I went to buy a copy of the 'Picnic' soundtrack off him and he said he'd heard I'd edited Pantosphinx for Liverpool University and would I be interested in working on a magazine for Frank Hessy, the music store. Allan, of course, knew we were art students and asked us to help out on an Arts Ball he was organising at St George's Hall.

He was later to ask Stuart and Rod to paint some murals in the club as the two of them had mentioned they'd painted murals for Ye Cracke pub and the Norris Green Territorial Army barracks. I was there but I have no recollection of John Lennon taking part, although Rod Jones lent an occasional hand. It's obvious that the murals bear no resemblance to John's art or style, being more in Stuart's vein.

I asked Rod for his memories and he told me: "The work I did by myself for Allan, no John or Stu involved, was the painting on the window shutters and that was the one that I was paid for in spirits!" (He didn't receive money, just a bottle of Vodka).

"One of the murals – I think that there were more than just the one – in the basement was done by Stu with I think John and Rod Jones input and I am sure that I played some part in one of them but I must say things are a little blurred and also get mixed up with later work in the Blue Angel. I am not quite sure of the date of the barracks but the image was 'bacchanalian'.

"The one in the Crack was a dock scene. Dick Edgerton later commissioned me to paint four oils of some of his other pubs and Diz and I went on our honeymoon on the strength of this windfall. In Gambier Terrace, Rod Jones and myself started a business called Murals. I still have our visiting cards! We did quite a few clubs and coffee bars in 1960/61."

So, basically, all these stories that the murals were painted by Stu and John are greatly exaggerated. Apparently, any help Stu had from John and Rod Jones was minimal but, because of John's name, the publicity has focussed on him while Stu's partner in the work, Rod Murray, hardly gets a mention.

Allan Williams co-presented a rock 'n' roll extravaganza at Liverpool Stadium, headlined by Gene Vincent, but featuring a lot of local groups, although John's group were never invited to participate. Stu then heard that Williams was arranging auditions for London impresario Larry Parnes at the nearby Wyvern Club with some of Liverpool's top bands and asked Allan if he could include them. As a result they were booked to back Johnny Gentle on a short Scottish tour. Since the resident steel band at the club had left to perform elsewhere, Williams asked the group if they could make some appearances in the small basement cellar, which they did during May.

Lord Woodbine and His Royal Caribbean Steel Band were a popular attraction in the Jacaranda cellar. When Woody left the band to open a club of his own, the remaining quartet, Everett, Otto, Bones and Slim, then simply called themselves the Royal Caribbean Steel Band. Williams was to comment, "The boys were so black and the Jac basement dance floor so dark, that you couldn't see them until they smiled."

One night Williams arrived at the club to discover that his star attraction hadn't turned up. They then wrote from Hamburg urging him to come over and book groups into the clubs there. Casey Jones of Cass & the Cassanovas always maintained that he used the Jacaranda phone to make calls to Bruno Koshmider in Germany late at night, after the club had closed, and that Allan answered the phone one day and took over the contact. If this were true it may explain how the Royal Caribbean Steel Band found themselves in the German port. Could they have answered a call from Hamburg and found they had talked themselves into a gig?!

Williams urgently needed a band to fill the vacuum and he decided to book the Silver Beetles for a series of appearances, beginning on 30 May 1960 for a relatively low fee.

This was around the time that I met Virginia there. We used to watch the Silver Beetles in the cellar with Cynthia and Dot Rhone sitting on chairs facing the group, holding broom handles to which the mics were attached. Then, when Virginia and I often left the Jacaranda to go to Streates, we'd see John necking Cynthia, and Paul necking Dot in the Slater Street doorways.

When their drummer Tommy Moore left the group following a gig at the Jacaranda coffee bar on Monday 13 June of that year, the Beatles were desperate for a replacement. They were pondering

over the problem one night while sitting in the coffee bar when they heard the sound of drumbeats from across the street. Almost directly opposite the Jacaranda in Slater Street was a picture-framing establishment. Norman Chapman worked there as a picture-framer and renovator, and played drums as a hobby, practising on a hire-purchase kit in the offices of the firm in the evenings.

They went into the street, trying to find where the sound was coming from. They knocked on the doors of the National Cash Register Office and Chapman popped his head out of an upstairs window of the building. They offered him the position of drummer with the band. Chapman, an imposing six-foot-two in height, accepted the job.

However, he only managed to appear with them on three Saturday night gigs at the Grosvenor Ballroom, Birkenhead, on 18 and 25 June and 2 July, before he was called up for National Service and was conscripted for two years in Kenya and Kuwait. In later years he was to say that he did not regret being 'called up'.

Chapman established his own picture-framing business in Southport. He continued playing drums and was a member of a trio when he died of lung cancer in July 1995 at the age of 58.

His daughter Lillian has donated Norman's drum kit to the Jacaranda, where it is displayed. I only ever painted one portrait in oils and that was of Virginia – and Chapman was the person who framed it.

At the time when John, Stuart, Rod and I first used to hang around at the club, Allan sported a big black beard, which he later shaved off. It was at the Jacaranda that I asked John to write a piece on the group for me and he mentioned "a man with a beard cut off" – that refers to Allan.

Over the years the club has closed and re-opened several times. At one time it was turned into a late-night drinking club called the Maxie San Suzie. Then, following the death of John Lennon and the subsequent upsurge of interest in the Beatles, it reverted back to its original name. The premises has been extended into an additional building, has changed quite dramatically from the original coffee bar and now serves alcoholic drinks and is decorated with Beatles' photographs and memorabilia.

Murals in the Jacaranda, painted by
Stuart Sutcliffe and Rod Murray

Ged Fleming

Bill Harry

Mersey Beat founder Bill Harry
and his wife Virginia

"SOON AFTER THE
JACARANDA COFFEE
CLUB OPENED, JOHN,
STUART, ROD AND I
BECAME REGULARS."

93

SEEL STREET

On 10 May 1960 this was the site of the Wyvern Club, a former social club which had now been taken over by Allan Williams.

Allan had originally inked in a co-promotion at Liverpool Stadium with London impresario Larry Parnes featuring Eddie Cochran and Gene Vincent. Tragically, Cochran was killed in a road accident before the concert could take place.

The event was re-arranged at the same venue on Tuesday 3 May 1960, with Gene Vincent topping the bill. Apart from acts such as Italy's Nero & His Gladiators and American singer Davy Jones, there were a number of Liverpool acts featured including Rory Storm & the Hurricanes, Jerry (sic) & the Pacemakers, Cass & the Cassanovas and Lance Fortune.

John Lennon was among the members of the audience. Although Allan knew John and Stuart because they not only hung around the Jacaranda with Rod Murray and myself, but had helped to build floats for him at St George's Hall, it's possible he wasn't aware that they were part of a group at that time as he'd booked a number of local bands to appear.

Larry Parnes, who managed Liverpool star Billy Fury, was quite impressed with the Liverpool acts and back at the Jacaranda he asked Allan if he could set up an audition of some local groups as he was looking for bands to back his artists, particularly Fury. A few days later Allan received a letter from Parnes' personal assistant Mark Forster in which he stated: "Duffy Power will be touring Scotland from June 2nd to 11th inclusive and Johnny Gentle will be touring Scotland from June 16th to 25th. For these two periods, as agreed, we are willing to pay your groups £120 plus the fares from Liverpool.

"Should you agree to these suggestions we will arrange for both Duffy and Johnny, who incidentally is a Liverpool boy, to travel up to Liverpool to rehearse with your groups towards the end of May."

Forster continues: "We will make arrangements for Mr Parnes to come and audition your groups to select the most suitable. He will also bring Billy Fury as Billy will want one of these four groups for his own personal use. Incidentally, the idea of Billy wanting a group from his own home town will provide several interesting press stories and publicity tie-ups."

The four acts Allan booked for the audition, which he arranged to take place at his newly-acquired club, were Cass & the Cassanovas, Derry & the Seniors, Gerry & the Pacemakers and Cliff Roberts & the Rockers. He hadn't booked John's group, but Stuart approached Allan to tell him they had a group called the Silver Beetles who wanted to appear at the audition, so they became a last minute extra. Whether Allan knew of John's group at the time is conjecture as he never booked them for his Arts Ball, the Liverpool Stadium or among the original four groups selected for the audition.

Rory Storm & the Hurricanes, rated as one of Liverpool's leading bands, didn't audition because they had their own lead singer in Rory, who obviously wouldn't have stood to be replaced as vocalist in his own band. (If it were actually a fact that a band was to be chosen to back Billy Fury, what would Gerry Marsden, Derry Wilkie and Cliff Roberts do if their bands were chosen?)

Rory turned up at the audition, of course, as he was aware of the photo opportunity of him having a picture taken with Billy Fury. John was also to request Fury's autograph.

At the auditions, when it came time for the Silver Beetles to play, their drummer Tommy Moore hadn't turned up. Johnny Hutchinson of the Big Three was asked to sit in and reluctantly did so. Then Moore arrived and joined them.

It seems that Parnes decided not to select a group to back Fury – even though Fury actually seemed to prefer the Silver Beetles. However, he selected some of the groups to back his other artists, with the Silver Beetles booked to back Johnny Gentle on a short Scottish tour.

This audition actually set off events which led Williams to book groups into Hamburg. Derry & the Seniors were booked to support Johnny Gentle and they gave up their jobs and turned professional. Then the tour was cancelled. Naturally upset, Howie Casey and Derry Wilkie confronted Allan, who promised to make amends by taking them down to London to appear at the Two I's coffee bar in Old Compton Street. When they arrived, they were given a spot, at no fee, by Tom Littlewood. In the audience, over

Paul McCartney,
John Lennon and Rory Storm

from Hamburg and seeking another group to play at his Kaiserkeller club was Bruno Koschmider. He had already been to the 2 I's on an earlier occasion seeking a band for his club and booked the Jets, a group with the guitarist Tony Sheridan. He'd returned to London to find another band, watched Derry & the Seniors on stage and decided to book them.

So the Liverpool connection at this stage was purely a coincidence. Koschmider had been told London was where it all happened and this was the only city he went to find a group for his club. It was just a coincidence that Derry & the Seniors happened to be playing – and that was the spark that set fire to the Hamburg/Liverpool scene.

As for the audition for Parnes, a few myths were born here. Allan says that Stuart was such a bad bass player that he played with his back to the audience. Cheniston Roland actually took a series of more than 14 shots of the occasion, with photos of both drummers with the group – Hutchinson and Moore. There were several photos with Stuart present, but Allan decided to put the one where he was tuning his guitar with his back to the photographer in his book. In other photos he is seen openly

"LARRY PARNES, WHO MANAGED LIVERPOOL STAR BILLY FURY, WAS QUITE IMPRESSED WITH THE LIVERPOOL ACTS."

"STUART APPROACHED ALLAN TO TELL HIM THEY HAD A GROUP CALLED THE SILVER BEETLES WHO WANTED TO APPEAR AT THE AUDITION, SO THEY BECAME A LAST MINUTE EXTRA"

standing facing the audience – as he's seen in other photos taken in Hamburg. However, Allan claims that Parnes wanted to hear them play without Stuart, which John refused, leading Parnes to decide not to have them back Billy Fury. Parnes himself denied this. He said that he decided against them because the drummer Tommy Moore turned up late, was dressed differently from the others and was a lot older than them.

Due to what Allan said, Stuart has gone down in history as an atrocious guitarist who played with his back to the audience.

When we used to book the group for the art college dances, there seemed no problem with Stuart's performance. I remember once in the room at the back of the canteen stage, Stuart proudly showed me the new guitar he'd just obtained from Hessy's, handed it to me and I tried to strum on it and found that the skin had come off my fingers! I hadn't realized I needed a plectrum! In fact, I never heard any criticism of Stuart as a musician until the publication of Williams' book.

Pauline Sutcliffe, Stuart's younger sister, told me that Stuart had had piano lessons, along with the rest of the family, and his father had brought him an acoustic guitar from Spain as a present some years before. Stuart, who had always been interested in music and art, was a big Presley fan. When he obtained his bass guitar from Frank Hessy's he began to practice to Elvis records on his tiny record player and had David May, a fellow art student who was in a local group the Silhouettes, teach him how to play the Eddie Cochran number 'C'mon Everybody'. May also began to coach him on further numbers.

Pauline said that from letters she received and what people told her, Stuart was a popular performer in Hamburg, and a highlight of the Beatles' act was Stuart's solo on 'Love Me Tender'. He left the Beatles for reasons other than his musical ability, but still hungered for the stage and actually joined a German rock group, the Bats, for a few weeks to fill in for their absent bassist, shortly before his death.

She also told me that he was a better musician than history remembers him, commenting, "I don't think he was as outstandingly bad as he's been described, because none of them were excellent, were they, until they went to Hamburg and started to play." She added, "George was better, Paul was better, but nothing like the musicians they became. I mean, they were just more competent, but according to Stuart's letters, and conversations with him, he thought himself good enough to do session work after he left them and I've got the letters, he was asked to be in other groups."

I talked to Rick Hardy (aka Richards), who was a member of the first British rock band to appear in Hamburg, the Jets. The Beatles performed on some sessions with the Jets on their first trip and when I told him what Allan had written in his book, he said:

Allan Williams at The Blue Angel on Seel Street

"What's the matter with this guy? Stu never turned his back on stage. I remember him as he played 'Matchbox', appearing a lonely figure on stage, dressed like James Dean. He certainly played to the audience and he certainly played bass. If you have someone who can't play the instrument properly, you have no bass sound. There were two rhythm guitarists with the Beatles and if one of them couldn't play, you wouldn't have noticed it - but it's different with a bass guitar.

"I was there and I can say quite definitely, Stuart never did a show in which he wasn't facing the audience."

When the group was playing in Liverpool and Hamburg, there seemed to be no complaints about Stuart's ability in the group. Howie Casey, leader of the first Liverpool band to play in Hamburg, Derry & the Seniors, was topping the bill at the Kaiserkeller while the Beatles were playing at the Indra. Promoter Bruno Koschmider decided to have another band during the interval at the Kaiserkeller rather than a jukebox, so he split up the Beatles and the Seniors and another outfit was formed with Casey on sax, Stan Foster on piano, Stuart on bass and a German modern jazz drummer. If Stu couldn't play, Casey certainly wouldn't have tolerated him in this outfit.

Next we come to Klaus Voormann, who was to become a famous bass guitarist appearing with numerous bands over the years and making several records backing each of the solo Beatles and once considered to replace Paul.

Klaus said, "He (Stu) was a really good bass player, a very basic bass player, completely different. So basic that you could say he was, at the time, my favourite bass player, but primitive. But of all the people or groups, and when we saw groups later, he was my favourite bass player."

It was Stuart who first began to show Klaus the basics of playing bass guitar.

Klaus was also to comment: "The Beatles were best when Stuart was still in the band. They played more or less the same repertoire later, and they played it good, but to me it had more balls, it was even more rock 'n' roll when Stuart was playing the bass and Paul was playing piano or another guitar. The band was somehow, as a rock 'n' roll band, more complete."

What happens when a seed is planted in a book like Williams' is that the story grows, and in all subsequent books, mainly by people who never knew him or witnessed his performances, the same story that he couldn't play the bass and performed with his back to the audience is trotted out.

Repeat a story enough times and even some people involved begin to believe it. The mud sticks.

For example, Paul McCartney, many years later, was to say, "The problem with Stu was that he couldn't play bass guitar. We had to turn him away in photographs because he'd be doing F-sharp and we'd be holding G."

(It's interesting to note Paul's comments about Stuart literally decades after his death. Yet, if we ignore hindsight and go back to what Paul felt at the time. He had a completely different opinion. In a 1964 interview in Beat Instrumental, in which he was discussing guitars, Paul commented, "I believe that playing an ordinary guitar first and then transferring to bass has made me a better bass player because it loosened up my fingers. NOT that I'm suggesting that EVERY bass player should learn on ordinary guitar. Stuart Sutcliffe certainly didn't, and he was a great bass man.")

It's not unusual for someone to report on their experiences or opinions and then years later, perhaps through hindsight, a faulty memory or by being influenced by what they have read, to come out with something that completely contradicts their previous statements.

Initially, all the local musicians were self-taught and in various stages of ability. Paul himself made a hash of it at the New Clubmoor Hall on 18 October 1959, when he attempted to play lead guitar. He played an abominable version of 'Guitar Boogie' and ended his one and only stint at playing lead.

Yet George Harrison would seem to have a different point of view regarding Stu's ability.

When the group returned to Liverpool following their Hamburg debut, Stuart stayed behind and they recruited Chas Newby to appear at three gigs with them. Then, until Stuart returned, Paul took over on bass.

The Blue Angel club on Seel Street

George had refused to become the group's bass guitarist and wrote to Stuart in Hamburg, "Come home sooner, as if we get a new bass player for the time being, it will be crumby as he will have to learn everything. It's no good with Paul playing bass, we'd decided, that is if he had some kind of bass and amp to play on!"

If Stuart was such a hopeless player as many people who never knew him or saw him maintain, why would George be so anxious to have him back in the group?

Allan changed the name of the Wyvern club to the Blue Angel as his dream was to operate a sophisticated night club. He'd visited the Blue Angel club in London and decided on adopting the title, decorating the main stairway with a huge blow-up of Marlene Dietrich from 'The Blue Angel' film.

The Blue opened on 22 March 1961 with cabaret artist Alma Warren, backed by the Terry Francis Quartet. The club achieved a degree of media attention because Allan granted membership to his friends at the Press Club, in particular to Bill Marshall the local rep for the Daily Mirror newspaper.

Press stories included the tale of the female snake charmer who lost her snake at the club – and the real bullfighting sessions which took place with a baby bull.

The Beatles and ourselves weren't initially granted membership as Allan didn't want elements of the local music scene around – he was trying to build an affluent and sophisticated clientele, plus he was still upset that the Beatles hadn't paid him a percentage of their Top Ten Club season in Hamburg, which had actually been arranged by Pete Best.

Virginia and I managed to get our membership by helping local sculptor Arthur Dooley arrange his exhibition there. Arthur, a 6ft 4in, active member of the Communist Party, who had the habit of not wearing his dentures, was given space in the front first floor room to hold his exhibition. Once we'd set all the pieces up, Arthur discovered a gap in the corner of the room. He marshalled us out and the three of us wandered down Seel Street while Arthur sought inspiration. We came to a debris and he had us pick up a huge wooden beam which we carted back to the Blue. Arthur stuck it against the wall, whitewashed it and priced the 'sculpture' at £250!

The club didn't succeed as a cabaret venue and Alan dropped his veto on the Beatles and other groups. By that time Virginia and I had launched Mersey Beat and the local rock 'n' roll scene was now attracting attention.

For the next few years the Blue became one of the most

Gerry Marsden with the Beatles

"THE BLUE BECAME ONE OF THE MOST INTERESTING CLUBS IN THE WORLD, CROWDED WITH MEMBERS OF GROUPS WHO'D ARRIVE SHORTLY BEFORE MIDNIGHT AFTER FINISHING GIGS AROUND THE CITY."

interesting clubs in the world. Initially the place was crowded with members of groups who'd arrive shortly before midnight after finishing gigs around the city. Other showbiz personalities such as Tommy Steele, the Bachelors and Bruce Forsyth dropped by when they were in Liverpool.

Playwright Alun Owen told us he regularly visited Liverpool from his home in Wales to recharge his batteries. He had an 'ear' for dialogue and used to carry a notebook to jot down the phrases he heard, examples of the famous Scouse wit.

In fact, the Blue was the setting for the after-the-show party when 'Maggie May' made its debut in Manchester. We all drove back to Liverpool and poured into the Blue. On the ground floor there was a grand piano, with fruit machines on either side. I was playing one of the machines with Judy Garland and she told me she'd like to sing – could I find someone to play the piano. No problem, I thought, with a club full of musicians - but no one would volunteer (despite 'Over The Rainbow' being one of the songs in several Mersey group repertoires), so we missed the golden opportunity of a special performance from Judy. As the night progressed Allan had an argument with the legendary singer and told her to leave the club and never darken its doors again!

I'd become friendly with the Rolling Stones soon after the Beatles had visited them in Richmond and when I heard they were playing in Southport, phoned their hotel, told Mick I was in the Blue and invited them down. They drove over from Southport in their van, with their equipment, and got up on stage and gave us a show.

The Blue was a compact club, entered through a large copper-coloured door, guarded by a bouncer. The ground floor had a

grand piano, various fruit machines and a corner bar, with a door leading onto a patio. The basement featured a larger bar, a stage and the gent's toilet. The first floor sported two rooms, one with a large statue of a nude woman, the other with Sans souci, a casino run by Barry Chang, Alan's brother-in-law. The second floor harboured the ladies room and an office.
Live entertainment was provided by resident bands and there were regular jam sessions.

John Lennon and I usually drank in the downstairs bar. At one time I asked him if he had a song he could give to Beryl Marsden, a 15-year-old singer who was Liverpool's equivalent of Brenda Lee. He said he had one in mind, 'Love of the Loved'. Next time I asked him about it he was apologetic – Brian Epstein had told him that as manager he would decide who would be given the Lennon & McCartney songs and he wanted to use them for his own stable.

John Lennon was also going out with another girl, Ida Holly, while he kept his marriage to Cynthia a secret. On a couple of occasions Virginia and I shared a cab with them on our way home, with John dropping Ida off near her home in the Sefton Park area. At this time there was no sign of Cynthia and we thought John was no longer going out with her. We weren't aware that she was pregnant at the time. The affair with Ida didn't last because her father objected to John.

Ida was a pretty girl with raven black hair who I arranged to be a compere at the Majestic Ballroom and on an Isle of White cruise. She left for London to share a flat with Marie Gurion while John was finding comfort with another girl Patricia Inder.

Saturday Evening Post writer Al Aronowitz had introduced Virginia and me to the work of his friend Bob Dylan. When Dylan arrived in Britain for a tour we attended his reception in London. Dylan and I became involved in a long chat and I took him to a phone booth in the hotel and got John Lennon on the phone and arranged for Dylan to visit him at his home. Dylan asked me to show him around Liverpool following his concert appearance at the Odeon.

Virginia and I went to the Adelphi Hotel after the show and he asked us up to his room where he introduced us to his manager Al Grossman and we began chatting about Liverpool poets, a poetry-to-jazz concert I'd organised, and how Liverpool poets had their own outlook, which was different to that of the Beat poets of San Francisco.

He then asked if we could take him out to meet some of the poets, so we went down to the Blue where we met poet Roger McGough and his Scaffold mate Mike McGear (McCartney). Bob was disappointed to discover that the Blue didn't sell Beaujolais and suggested we return to the hotel, inviting some friends to join us. We went back with Roger, Mike and a trio of girl singers, the Poppies, who were managed by Roger at the time. Later, I heard that Dylan had invited the Poppies down to London and produced a record with them, although I don't recall it ever being released.

In the first issue of Mersey Beat I'd written a feature on a local singer Priscilla White, but had mistakenly called her Cilla Black. She told me she preferred the 'Black' and continued to call herself by that name.

One night when Cilla was down at the Blue with her mate Pat Davies I noticed that Brian Epstein was present, sitting under the basement stairs with Andrew Loog Oldham. I asked Cilla if she'd get up and sing and arranged for the Masterminds, the group on stage to back her performing the number 'Boys'. Then I asked Brian to listen to her and when she finished the song I brought her over and introduced her to him, and then left them to have a chat. The

next day she phoned me to say that she'd had a meeting with Brian and he'd agreed to manage her.

There were various resident bands who played at the Blue, including the Escorts (at the time Ringo Starr's cousin was in the band and it was Ringo who arranged their residency) and the Nocturnes. Alun Owen liked the Nocturnes and they were hired to appear as the Beat group in the stage musical.

Another friend of ours, Geoff Hughes, who worked as a salesman in the car showroom next to the Mersey Beat office, also managed to get a part in 'Maggie May'. Geoff then went on to have a successful acting career (he was the voice of Paul McCartney in 'Yellow Submarine') as Eddie Yates in 'Coronation Street' and in 'Keeping Up Appearances', 'The Royle Family' and 'Heartbeat'.

Each night there were up to thirty members of the various local groups down at the Blue. There were always lots of girls. I remember Rory Storm and Ringo Starr with two girls, who looked like twins with their jet black fringed hair – Ringo was to marry one of them, Maureen Cox. Cilla and her mate Pat were regulars, as was Marie Gurion, who later married Justin Hayward of the Moody Blues.

Apart from the Beatles, regulars included the Bluejeans, the Hurricanes, Freddie Starr, Billy Kramer, Mark Peters, the Dennisons, the Chants, the Big Three, the Undertakers, the Searchers, Derry Wilkie, Howie Casey, the Hillsiders, the Mojos and Faron's Flamingos.

At one time Allan used the lid of the grand piano as a 'board of fame', getting all celebrity visitors to sign it – I wonder what happened to it?
By the end of the 1960s, the Angel was closed, but was reopened as a drinking club under various names. In recent years the club re-adopted the name Blue Angel and plays host to guests at the annual Mersey Beatles convention.

John Lennon, Paul McCartney, George Harrison and Ringo Starr pictured during takes for the film 'A Hard Day's Night' in 1964

CHAPTER 8
LIFE AND DEATH

SEFTON GENERAL HOSPITAL

This is the hospital, situated in Smithdown Road, Liverpool 15 where John's mother Julia was taken following the accident in Menlove Avenue in which she was run down. This event, on 15 July 1958, was to haunt John throughout the rest of his life.

Once a week Julia usually visited her sister Mimi's house in Menlove Avenue, where John still lived, although on this particular evening he was at her home in Blomfield Road. Julia was chatting with Mimi until ten o'clock in the evening and then Julia left to cross Menlove Avenue to the bus stop. Mimi generally walked to the bus stop with her, but decided not to that night.

As Julia came out of the garden gate she met Nigel Walley, John's friend, who had come looking for him. They stopped to talk for a moment and then she stepped to cross to the central reservation when a car crashed into her sending her hurtling into the air. She died instantly. A police officer, who was late for duty and was also driving without a licence, had been speeding along the road. He was an inexperienced driver and when he saw Julia he put his foot on the accelerator instead of the brake.

Julia was only 44.

John was at the Blomfield Road house with Bobbie Dykins, Julia's partner, while Julia went to visit Mimi. Later that evening a policeman knocked on the door and informed them that Julia had been killed in an accident.

John was to recall the incident in detail years later, saying, "An hour or so after it happened a copper came to the door to let us know about the accident. It was awful, like some dreadful film where they ask you if you're the victim's son and all that. Well, I was, and I can tell you it was absolutely the worst night of my entire life.

"I lost my mother twice, once as a child of five and then again at seventeen. It made me very, very bitter inside. I had just begun to re-establish a relationship with her when she was killed. We'd caught up on so much in just a few short years. We could communicate. We got on. Deep down inside, I thought, 'Sod it! I've no real responsibilities to anyone now.

"Anyway, Bobbie and I got a cab over to Sefton General Hospital where she was lying dead. I remember rabbiting on hysterically to the cabbie all the way there. Of course, there was no way I could ever bear to look at her. Bobbie went in to see her for a few minutes, but it turned out to be too much for the poor sod and he finally broke down in my arms out in the lobby. I couldn't seem to cry, not then anyway, I suppose I was just frozen inside."

When he left the hospital, John returned to Menlove Avenue and began playing his guitar. Then later that night he walked down the road to his former girlfriend, Barbara Baker's house. They walked to a nearby park and he started to cry and she placed her arms around him. She said, "We just stood there, crying our eyes out, the pair of us."

John never got over his mother's death and recorded songs such as 'Julia' and 'Mother' about her.
He was finally able to externalise some of his feelings when he underwent primal therapy and also in recording his album 'John Lennon/Plastic Ono Band.' He also named his son Julian after her.

Bobby Dykins couldn't cope with Julia's death and, since he also worked such long and unsociable hours that it would have proved difficult to bring up his daughters, Julia and Jacqui went to live with their Aunt Harriet.

 is captioned with: Nigel Walley, manager of the Quarry Men, who Julia stopped to talk to shortly before her fatal accident in 1958

Nigel Walley

1958: Julia Lennon is hit by a car and killed

1963: Julian Lennon is born

Bobby couldn't bear to remain alone in Blomfield Road and moved out a few weeks later. He only lived half a mile away from the girls and they visited each other regularly.

After a time Dykins met and married a woman called Roda. Then, in 1966, another tragedy occurred. Bobby and Roda had been visiting friends in Ruthin, North Wales and drove back to Liverpool one rainy night. When they entered Penny Lane their car skidded and crashed into a lamppost. Rona sustained minor injuries, but Bobby was taken to Sefton General Hospital where he later died from his injuries. His daughter says the accident occurred in 1966.

Julian Lennon was born here at 7.45am on Monday, 8 April 1963. After Cynthia had experienced labour pains while she'd been shopping, she asked her best friend Phyllis McKenzie to stay overnight with her in Mendips. Cynthia cried out in pain once she'd gone to bed and Phyllis phoned for an ambulance. The two girls were taken to Sefton General Hospital dressed only in their nightdresses, protected from the cold by their dressing gowns.

Describing the birth, Cynthia was to write, "He was beautiful. The reason for the difficulty during Julian's birth was because the umbilical chord was wrapped around his neck, he arrived into this world an awful yellow colour, apart from that he was perfect, just perfect."

John, who had been touring, arrived at Sefton General a week later. By this time, Cynthia, who had initially been placed in a public ward, had been moved into a private room costing 25 shillings a day.

When John arrived he was delighted and exclaimed: "Who's going to be a famous little rocker like his Dad then?"

105

AFTERWORD

Of course, there were so many other Liverpool places and people with an association to John.

Litherland Town Hall, where the Beatles made such a spectacular appearance on 28 December 1960; the Tower Ballroom gigs, attended by thousands of Merseyside youth; the Nems office; Horne Brothers where the Beatles had their hair styled; the Empire Theatre where idols such as Buddy Holly and Lonnie Donegan appeared and where Brian Epstein took them to show them the Shadows bowing at the end of their act – a lesson he insisted they follow; the Grapes pub in Mathew Street, and so on.

Lots of people too – how John stopped Brian Epstein firing Frieda Kelly and how she then became their fan club secretary; Bob Wooler, the Cavern disc jockey who wrote such a prophetic article about the Beatles in Mersey Beat.

In fact, the Mersey Beat office was a regular haunt for John and the newspaper was responsible for his first published work. John also gave me approximately 250 stories and drawings saying they were mine to do with what I wished, so I created the name Beatcomber and began publishing the works as separate items – they became the inspiration for his books. He would sometimes come into the office with Cynthia and we would go down to the Coffee Pot for bacon, egg and beans. Steve Day recalled how he was in the Mersey Beat office when John came bounding up the stairs, leapt over the counter and began throwing papers in the air. He would dig deep into his pockets to see if he could afford to take out some bizarre classified ads – yes, there are so many memories of John.

I hope the few examples I have presented in this book will give some idea of the excitement of the times and perhaps an insight into John himself and how the city helped to develop the youth who became one of the major 20th century icons.

Left: John Lennon and George Harrison with James Rushworth at Rushworths music store in Whitechapel, Liverpool

Above: Bill Harry presents The Beatles with their 'No. 1 Group On Merseyside' award at the Majestic Ballroom, Birkenhead in December 1961

Imagine

Imagine there's no heaven
It's easy if you try
No hell below us
Above us only sky
Imagine all the people
living for today....

Imagine there's no countries
it isn't hard to do
nothing to kill or die for
and no religion too
imagine all the people
living life in peace....

John Lennon's original orange-tinted spectacles on show at the Beatles Story in Liverpool

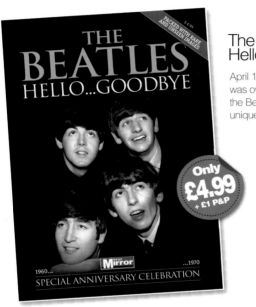

The Beatles: Hello ... Goodbye

April 10, 1970 and the dream was over. It's 40 years since the Beatles split up, but their unique legacy lives on.

Only £4.99 + £1 P&P

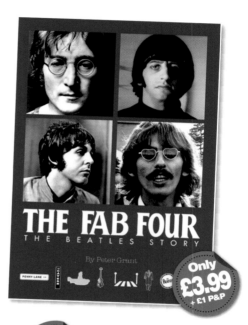

The Fab Four: The Beatles Story

The origins and careers of John, Paul, George and Ringo – four lads who became icons of music, fashion, film and culture.

Only £3.99 + £1 P&P

Bigger Than The Beatles

Liverpool has always been a hub of talent – this is the story of the city's musical odyssey.

Only £6.75 FREE P&P

Only £6.75 FREE P&P

The McCartneys: In The Town Where They Were Born

Roll up – and that's an invitation – to find all about the real Sir Paul McCartney and the secrets of his childhood and early life in Liverpool.

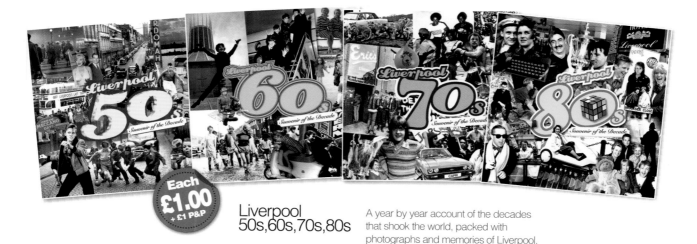

Each £1.00 + £1 P&P

Liverpool 50s, 60s, 70s, 80s

A year by year account of the decades that shook the world, packed with photographs and memories of Liverpool.

Only £16.00 + £2.50 P&P

Beatles Liverpool T-shirt

Artistic white image on black t-shirt of the Fab Four above the Liverpool Skyline.

Only £280.00 + £20.00 P&P

John Lennon bronze

Cold-cast bronze, by the artist behind the Lennon statue at Liverpool John Lennon Airport. The statue is 16" tall, 7" wide and 7" deep.

Only £7.99 + £2.50 P&P

Beatles Mug

An iconic image of the Beatles return to Liverpool in 1964 for the premiere of their film, A Hard Day's Night.

John Lennon Imagine bust

Depicts a classic image of his 'Imagine' days. Available in cold-cast bronze or pewter, it is 7" tall, 4" wide and 3" deep.

Only £66.00 + £10.00 P&P

Trinity Mirror Media